PRAYER AND CONTEMPLATION

PRAYER AND CONTEMPLATION

ROBERT LLEWELYN

SLG PRESS
Convent of the Incarnation
Fairacres, Oxford

ISBN   0   7283   0040   0

PREFACE

'Mystical experience is given to some. But contemplation is for all Christians. Allow me to say a word about that prayer which is indeed for all of us. . . . [It] means essentially our being with God, putting ourselves in his presence, being hungry and thirsty for him, wanting him, letting heart and mind and will move towards him; with the needs of the world on our heart. It is a rhythmic movement of the personality into the eternity and peace of God, and no less for the turmoil of the world for whose sake as for ours, we are seeking God. If that is the heart of prayer then the contemplative part of it will be large. And a Church which starves itself and its members in the contemplative life deserves whatever spiritual leanness it may experience.'

The quotation is from Archbishop Ramsey,* and the passage gives a good general sense in which the word contemplation is used in this book. In this sense it is, I believe, an experience into which every committed Christian may at some stage expect to be drawn. A growing number today are looking to the Churches—and often beyond—to lead them to a new dimension in prayer. These pages are written in the conviction that the key to their search lies within the great tradition of Christian spirituality, and in the hope that many will find in them the encouragement and guidance which they seek.

* *Canterbury Pilgrim* by Michael Ramsey (SPCK 1974) pp. 59-60.

Acknowledgement

I am grateful to the Editor of *Christian* for permission to reprint the following chapters which have appeared in recent issues of that journal. The whole reproduces in substance the 1974 Lenten addresses in Canterbury Cathedral.

CONTENTS

Chapter 1

PRAYER AS PETITION

I propose to approach our subject of prayer from the angle of supplication, a word which describes prayer in all its petitionary and intercessory aspects. Supplication is basic to the very idea of prayer—the etymology of the word prayer alone suggests that—and it is, I believe, the way we come to prayer, and an indispensable form of prayer in one way or another throughout our lives. When the disciples asked Jesus to teach them how to pray he gave them as their model a prayer which is petitionary in form from beginning to end. It is true that it is placed in the setting of adoration, as all supplication to God should be; the first request is that God's name be kept holy. And it is true also that the petition is never for selfish personal ends; the corporate aspect of the prayer is safeguarded throughout by the first two words 'Our Father', reminding us that we make our petitions as members of a family, regarding the needs of others as concernedly as our own. It is true, further, that our Lord's prayer lifts our sights far beyond our own small concerns, whether individual or corporate, beyond the horizons of family or community or parish or church or even nation. 'Thy kingdom come', we pray, 'thy will be done, as in heaven so on earth', thus projecting our desires to Ireland and the Middle East; to Russia and South Africa and all oppressed peoples; to India and the third world where poverty and destitution bring men and women to the brink of despair; as well as to our own country where the corroding power of affluence and prosperity is a constant threat to that foundation on which all true religion rests, the sense of trust and hope in God.

There is nothing parochial in petitions such as these. They embody the aspirations of very many people at this time, including many people who are out of touch with any form of organised religion, that the love of God

1

which is at the heart of the gospel committed to us shall find its due expression in political, social and economic justice. Only when these great issues are attended to are we allowed to look to our more immediate needs, 'give us this day our daily bread', still praying as members of a family—'us' and not 'me'—and asking for all things temporal and spiritual to enable us to fulfil God's purpose. We pass on to ask for the forgiveness of our sins, a petition which relates to our relationship with God as well as to one another; and then to the last petition, in which we ask God not to allow us to be tried beyond our strength, and to save us from evil in the testing fire of temptation. And so the Lord's Prayer is petitionary throughout (the doxology being not part of the original prayer, but an addition used by the early Church).

From the Lord's Prayer itself let us pass on to our Lord's direct teaching on prayer, and always we shall find that it is the petitionary aspect of prayer which is expounded. In St Luke's gospel the Lord's Prayer is immediately followed by the parable of the householder who through the untimely arrival of a guest goes at midnight to a friend's house to beg for food, and refuses to allow any peace to the man or his family until this request is granted. The almost parallel story of the unjust judge also calls for persistence in prayer. This time we have a widow pestering a judge until he attends to her needs and grants her the justice she is seeking. In the further parable of the Pharisee and the Publican it is once again petitionary prayer which is commended, the publican's cry that God will be merciful to him as a sinner. So too, in our Lord's most commonly quoted teaching on prayer, 'Ask and it shall be given you; seek and you shall find; knock and it shall be opened to you', petitionary prayer pure and simple is placed before us. After being reminded that God will give not less lavishly and lovingly than a human father, we are led to the climax that God will surely give the Holy Spirit to those who ask him.

When we turn from our Lord's teaching and consider his own prayers such as have been passed on to us, we find yet again that they are basically petitionary. He prays for the soldiers, 'Father forgive them for they do not know what they do', and for Peter, 'I have prayed for you that your faith does not fail'. He prays for the disciples that they may be sanctified through the truth, and for the Church 'that they may be one, as Father thou art in me and I in thee, that they also may be one in us'. Finally, we may recall the distress and anguish in Gethsemane, 'Father if it be possible let this cup pass from me' leading on to petition at its most costly and sacrificial level, 'Nevertheless not my will but thine be done'.

It would not, however, be true to say that all our Lord's communing with the Father of which we have record is petitionary in form. There is intimate and loving colloquy in the High Priestly prayer: 'And this is life eternal that they might know thee the only true God, and Jesus Christ whom thou hast sent. I have glorified thee on earth, I have finished the work that thou gavest me to do . . .' There is too the spontaneous outburst of thanksgiving recorded by St Matthew and St Luke, 'I thank thee Father, Lord of heaven and earth that thou hast hidden these things from the wise and prudent and revealed them unto babes, even so Father for it seemed good in thy sight'; and also non-petitionary in form is the commendation upon the cross, 'Father into thy hands I commend my spirit'. But none of this trustful and moving and loving communion with the Father is referred to in the gospels as prayer.

Perhaps when I say this, I shall be accused of special pleading, of making out a case where no such case exists. 'When you use the word prayer, at least for your present purpose', it may be said, 'you don't mean what we mean by prayer.' That may be quite true, and if the reader chooses prayer to mean what most people usually choose it to mean—praise, thanksgiving confession, loving colloquy with God, as well as supplication—I have no quarrel with him. Each of us is at liberty to define as he pleases. 'When I use a word', says Humpty Dumpty to Alice, 'it means just what I choose it to mean, no more no less.' All that I plead is that we recognise what we are doing. We are moving away from the restricted sense in which the gospel uses the word prayer, which is basically and fundamentally petitionary, even though set in a framework of adoration and thanksgiving.

And what I have said of the gospels is no less true of the epistles, where petition remains at the heart of prayer, though again purged of its lower elements and cleansed and ennobled by the fire of the Spirit. As an example of the grandeur and nobility to which such prayer may rise let us take this passage from St Paul's epistle to the Ephesians: 'I bow my knees before the Father from whom every family in heaven and on earth is named, that according to the riches of his glory he may grant you to be strengthened with might through his Spirit in the inner man, and that Christ may dwell in your hearts by faith; that you being rooted and grounded in love may be able to comprehend with all the saints what is the breadth and depth and length and height, and to know the love of God which passes knowledge and that you may be filled with all the fullness of God.'

The same is true of the Old Testament. We can agree with the commentaries when they say that prayer in the Old Testament can be understood to include widely every form of address to God whatever its character. This is strictly true. The psalm of Hannah for example is referred to as prayer, though in form it is entirely praise and thanksgiving. Furthermore in the book of Psalms we find at the end of Psalm 72, 'The prayers of David the son of Jesse are ended', and these words must refer to all aspects of prayer and communion which have gone before. Yet by and large (and the references would go into hundreds: there are seventy petitions in the 119th Psalm alone) we know that Old Testament prayer is petitionary in form, such as Solomon's prayer at the dedication of the temple, or Nehemiah's in its rebuilding after the exile.

Is the point I am making that prayer in the Bible is deeply rooted in petition an academic one only? If I believed that, I would not have spent so long labouring it. On the contrary, I believe this point to be of immense practical importance. For it seems to me that nothing less than personality in God is at stake. Once the concept of petition at the heart of prayer is surrendered, it will not be long before we relinquish the idea of God as personal. And that is a statement which could equally be put the other way round. The conception of God as Father and prayer as petitionary are no more separable than the obverse and converse sides of a coin. In parenthesis let me add that I am conscious, even as I use it, that the word 'personal' with reference to God is deplorably inadequate. I should prefer to use some such word as supra-personal, but I can no more conceive what that means than I can conceive of a fourth dimension or a beginning and end of time. We call God 'He'—and 'She' would do equally well because the pronoun is concerned with personality and not sex—not because we mean 'he' in the sense in which we use this word of a friend, but because the limitation of language offers the personal pronoun as the only alternative to 'it'. If God were IT, IT with capital letters so that he were the greatest of all possible its, we should be his master, and not he ours. The pronoun 'He' can do no more than express that God has no less initiative than we have, even though we shall believe that he has vastly more. The doctrine of the Trinity, in itself a mystery, encourages us to think that a conception of the Godhead beyond the personal as we know it is not without meaning.

But to return. Once we lose the conception of personality as applied to God it will not be long before we lose the conception of him as absolute

4

demand, and so, on our side, of total commitment. That probably is the danger of what is generally called mystical religion when it is divorced from biblical theology. I think one has seen this in the East, where the biblical insights which we have just been considering are largely foreign. And I think we see it too in some esoteric cults which spring up in the West today, orientated around some guru or maharishi. The practice of religion becomes a matter of preference, like the choice of friends, and there is lacking the note of urgency, still more of obligation, which is stamped on the prophetic and dominical approach. I am not of course meaning to belittle mystical prayer—it is indeed in the silence we generally come to the heart of prayer—but simply stressing the importance of our prayer being based on biblical foundations. Thomas Merton has written: 'The simplicity of the gospels if kept in mind makes false mysticism impossible. Christ has delivered us for ever from the esoteric and the strange. He has brought the light of God to our own level to transfigure our ordinary existence.'

Readers of this book will, I suppose, fall into three main groups. There will be a few who do not believe in God, and to them it can have nothing to say, for prayer to a being who by hypothesis does not exist is a concept without meaning. There will be others who conceive of God in terms which deny personality, regarding him (let the personal pronoun stand) as a sort of diffused impersonal spiritual energy pervading the universe. It seems to follow that for such people prayer as we have regarded it can have no place. They might, I think, hope to use God, that is to say to harness this vast source of spiritual energy for the benefit of themselves and others; but to beseech him, to appeal to him, to invoke him—this would make no sense at all. You can harness the power of steam and use it for constructive ends in the propulsion of ships and trains, but you cannot make steam the object of a yearning and aspiring heart.

In the third group will be those of more or less orthodox Christian position, people who affirm personality within the Godhead, and who pray to God as Father. Yet amongst these it may be assumed there will be some who can find no place for petitionary prayer except perhaps to allow a certain psychological benefit to those who know they are being prayed for. Having in mind the difficulties of this class, let us go on to consider the objection they are likely to bring against petitionary prayer, and as we proceed, some of the values which are conserved within this realm of prayer will I think become clearer.

The objection would, I think, run on some such lines as these. 'I believe God', they would say, 'to be perfect wisdom and perfect love. If he is all wise he knows what is best. I should not like him to give what is second best whether for myself or anyone else, and if I prayed to him I might ask for just that. And, anyway, if he is all loving, surely he will give what is best without my asking him? Therefore I prefer to worship him, and to praise him, and to enter into silent communion with him, but not to ask him for anything whether for myself or others. I leave it to him to give what he sees best.' This may at first sight seem a not unreasonable argument, and it is not one presented or exclusively presented by lukewarm or shallow people. It was, for example, one of the points held against Madam Guyon in her examination by the Roman Catholic Church that her system of prayer allowed no place for petition or intercession.

The fallacy is that it considers two possibilities—if God wills it, it will happen anyway; and if God doesn't will it, I mustn't pray for it—and uses them as a reason for not praying. But the argument has overlooked a third possibility, that God may want this event to happen—this sick person, let us suppose, to recover—*in answer to our prayer.* Our line of reasoning has lost sight of the possibility that prayer may open a channel through which it becomes morally possible for God to work, not—as Fr Raynes of the Community of the Resurrection used to say—*changing* God's purpose, but *releasing* it. The thought will be made clearer if we transfer our attention from the realm of prayer to that of action. Here, then, is a mother with her baby boy whose life depends on being fed at her breast. She reasons thus: 'God wants my child to live or he does not. If he wants him to live he will live anyhow, and I need not feed him. If he doesn't want him to live, I should be wrong to feed him. Either way I do nothing.' The fallacy, painfully obvious in the realm of action, seems often to go undetected in the realm of prayer. God wants this child to live *through* the mother's co-operation, with all that this means to mother and child in establishing a relationship of dependence and love on which the healthy spiritual and psychological development of both depend. No basic change of principle is involved in God's ways of dealing with men in moving from the sphere of action to that of prayer.

What has been laboured perhaps unduly is summed up tersely by C. S. Lewis as follows: ' "Praying for particular things", said I, "always seems like advising God how to run the world. Wouldn't it be wiser to assume

6

that He knows best?" "On the same principle", said he, "I suppose you never ask the man next to you to pass the salt, because God knows best whether you ought to have salt or not. And I suppose you never take an umbrella, because God knows best whether you ought to be wet or dry." "That's quite different", I protested. "I don't see why", said he. "The odd thing is that He should let us influence the course of events at all. But since He lets us do it in one way, I don't see why He shouldn't let us do it in the other." '

Whether it be odd or not, it is certainly beyond dispute that God does allow us to change the course of the world by our hands and feet and brains, these physical organs being but three among many, which as instruments of the human will may modify the stream of events around us. When the atom bomb was dropped on Japan in 1945 bringing the war abruptly to its end, every country in the world felt in some measure the impact of that event. And God allowed this to come about through man, man's brain in designing this 'hideous strength', and through the members of his body in coordination with his mind and will. It is true that although God allows man an astonishing degree of freedom in shaping events for good or ill, yet that freedom is not absolute. Limitations are placed upon it, not necessarily for all time, for the domain under man's control progressively increases as nature yields up one secret after another. Where this will stop we have no means of knowing. Man can modify the weather by planting trees or cutting them down, or by firing chemicals into rain clouds, but he cannot control it to any extensive degree. Man can regulate the birth rate, but the sex of the unborn child is beyond his power to decide. The rise and fall of the ocean tide is also beyond his control. It is easy to see how disastrous human control in such things could be, and to be thankful that God in his wisdom has placed them and much else beyond our present powers. Yet these, and other examples we might take, perhaps serve only to remind us of the astonishing range of freedom which God allows. 'If then', the argument runs, 'God entrusts so much to us through the exercise of free will in the realm of action would it not be strange if he should entrust nothing in the realm of prayer?' We do not find any such division between action and speech—doing things and asking things—in ordinary family life. Each has its part to play in developing and deepening relationships in the home. The child will at one time express his heart's desire by action-playing cricket in the garden, romping with the dog, or making a model aeroplane—and at another time he

7

will express it by speech, asking his father if they may go camping for the summer holidays this year. The father will not always agree with his boy's request, but it is through the will being expressed in action and speech that family relations are developed and deepened. Our Lord encourages us to look to the family in discovering the manner of God's dealing with us, and nowhere is this more true than in the realm of prayer. It seems to me precisely as we would expect, that relationships which are proper within normal family life should have their counterpart amongst us who have received the spirit of adoption whereby we cry, 'Abba, Father'. It is the plain teaching of Jesus, that God our Father wants us in his love for us to look to him to supply our needs whether temporal or spiritual with the simplicity and faith of children, and to make known our requests boldly. It is true that he knows our needs before we ask him; we have our Lord's words for that. But prayer will prepare us to receive his gifts and use them in his service; fellowship and communion will be taken to new depths. And—a mark always of true discipleship—our lives will be irradiated by a spirit of thanksgiving. To make a request to God in prayer will not, of course, mean that we are excused from working as far as we may to bring about the end for which we have prayed. If our prayer is 'Create in me a clean heart O God and renew a right spirit within me', our lives must be as far as possible regulated to that end. Indeed the manner of our living will be the main test of the reality of our praying. We have taken for our example a prayer for spiritual blessing, but prayer for material blessing is equally enjoined in the New Testament (though all blessing, if it is indeed blessing, must be ultimately spiritual); and not only is it laid upon us in our Lord's teaching to pray for material blessings, but this duty is borne witness to in his healing miracles and other mighty works, and confirmed in the experience of men and women of all ages, and not least today.

What is it then I am saying? Is it that we may pray for anything we want? We may certainly *take* all our desires to God in prayer. It may be that God will grant them even when the things which we seek are not what we might call his primary will for us, just as a father might think it right to allow a headstrong schoolboy son to be out at night even though he knew the boy's best interest (which would be the father's primary will) lay in his remaining indoors and doing his homework. The Bible expresses that thought in Psalm 106, 'Lust came upon them in the wilderness and they tempted God in the desert. And he gave them their desire and sent leanness withal into their soul'. Colin Morris has expressed it still more tersely in the words, 'Look out what you pray for, you may get it', adding that if we judge from the mess we are in, many people's *real* prayers—meaning by 'real prayer' the heart's desire, and not necessarily the utterance of the lips—have indeed been granted. But, if we are trying to be realistic and sincere in our Christian living, our basic desire will not be that God will bend his will to ours, but that through the discipline of prayer our wills may be brought into conformity with his—that he will cleanse the defective desires of our hearts by the inspiration of the Holy Spirit. This, for the committed Christian, is a continuing process, and the Christian knows that at each stage what he looks to God for is likely to fall short of what God would have him receive, so every prayer is governed by the petition, 'thy will be done', whether explicitly expressed or not; which means that we are prepared, or more realistically, desire to be prepared, for anything, even if God's plans shall drive a deep furrow across our own. The anonymous writer of the words which follow must have been well schooled in the manner in which God is wont to deal with his people: 'So easily do we pray for the wrong things, for strength that we may achieve, and God gives us weakness that we may be humble; for health that we may do great things, and God gives us infirmity that we may do better things; for riches that we may be happy, and God gives us poverty that we may be wise; for power that we may have the praise of men, and God gives us weakness that we may feel the need of him; for all things that we may enjoy life, and God gives us life that we may enjoy all things; and so receiving nothing that we have asked for but all that we have genuinely hoped for, our prayer has been answered and we have been blessed.'

Although often we shall not know how to pray as we ought, we shall naturally seek to avoid what may be called the forbidden areas of prayer. Prayers which often seem permissible when we or others are viewed in isolation may become impossible when we reflect that we pray as members of a family in which the good of one may be in conflict with that of another. It is also important that our prayer shall specify 'open possibilities'. Here we are in some difficulty, but in practice all of us recognise that God has so ordered the world that some situations are open to prayer and others are closed. For example, most Christians would think it right to pray for a friend with a septic arm, the situation presuming an open possibility. If the arm had to be amputated we should say God had declared himself (at least in respect of his permissive will) and our prayer would be directed to our friend's mental adjustment to his new state. But it isn't easy to know what is open and what is closed. Sickness for example we should generally hold to be open; the weather, as another example, probably some would regard as open and many as closed; the timing of the ebb and flow of the tides we should all regard as closed. Only King Canute, so far as I know, thought differently! But it is important to observe that closed possibilities exist not because God's power is limited, but because if the world were otherwise organised and disciplined, life as we know it would become impossible.

Considerations such as these make petitionary prayer a very different thing from what people out of touch with the Church sometimes *imagine* Christians believe it to be—a sort of Aladdin's lamp which we can so manipulate as to bring about our fondest wish. If that picture were to have any resemblance to truth, the only condition under which chaos would not immediately ensue would be for the lamp itself to be in the hands of infinite wisdom and perfect love. And, hoping you will not press any of the details in this crude parable, for God is a master lover and not a master magician, that is just where we imagine the lamp to be; yet to affirm this does not exclude the possibility of God allowing man a certain freedom, consistent with human wisdom and love in the realm of petitionary prayer; but consistent also—the saving thought—with God's power to say 'no' as well as 'yes'.

I find it much easier to understand the man who denies absolutely the existence of God than the man who, believing in the God and Father of our Lord Jesus Christ, makes him deny to us cooperative activity in the realm of prayer. That prayer *does* effect new things; that certain events happen as a result of prayer being offered which would not otherwise have happened, Christians must surely believe beyond all doubt. Yet as we have seen, we need to balance this insight with another. We do not go to prayer that we may use God, but that he may use us. We trust him to use our prayer as he will, in the pursuit of his blessing, and also, we trust that, through the discipline and training of prayer, we might become more effective instruments of his will. One of the effects of prayer will be to fit us to receive aright the good things, spiritual and material, which God wants to give. And prayer for one another will build us up into a fellowship of love, the deepest of all God's blessings, from which much else will flow.

Perhaps one ought now to ask, what should be the manner of inter-cessory prayer?

Intercessory prayers such as we are familiar with in church have both advantages and dangers. Their advantages, as has well been said, are their richness, their theological depth, their spiritual insight, their balance and beauty of language, and their range so far beyond what our own prayers are likely to be. They give us a standard to which we may increasingly ap-proximate, setting before us things of lasting value in place of the transient things on which we so easily set our hearts. But these are values into which we have to grow. 'When I use the church's prayers', says Colin Morris, summing it all up in one colourful sentence, 'I feel like a small boy wearing his father's suit, hoping he will grow into it one day.'

But here, too, there is danger. Prayer is never just a matter of words. Its roots are in the desires of the heart. The act of speaking may often assist us in developing and expressing our inmost desires, but the words are a help to *us*, not to God. We should be warned also that words and phrases, however holy in their sound, cannot become prayer merely by being repeated. For prayer requires always an involvement of mind and heart and will. So long as this is present in relationship to God, there will be prayer offered, whether words are said or not. Conversely, no verbal utterance apart from such involvement can have the nature of prayer at all. When we pray as we are taught, 'Thy kingdom come', it will be for the perfect alone that words and desires are perfectly blended into one. For ourselves, our words will not so much express our desires as, rather, what we desire our desires shall be. We desire indeed that God's kingdom shall come, but we do not desire it as completely as we ought. If we put the energies of the soul into our words, fervently yet unaffectedly, then our words will help kindle our hearts, and bring utterance and desire into harmony. But there is a danger lest words, instead of being an expression of the interior energies of the spirit, become a substitute for it. If so, they turn to mockery: 'vain repetition', as our Authorised Version has it in a pregnant phrase. People sometimes think of 'vain repetition' as the saying over and over again of prayers like the Jesus Prayer; but, though repetition, this is often far from vain. The test is not in the repetition but in the depth and sincerity; a prayer repeated only once is vain repetition if our hearts are not also at prayer.

But what of intercessory prayer formulated in our own time, and our own choice of language; prayer made when we are alone with God? Should

11

our supplications be made with fervour and emotion, for example, or should they be calm, composed and serene? Should they for that matter be spoken aloud, or spoken silently in the mind? Or should they be expressed simply by the inclination of the heart? We cannot make a general rule, excepting to say that fervour and emotion should never be artificially worked up. If, as sometimes happens, we come to prayer with deep emotion in our hearts, then let it be; do not suppress it, except perhaps to lay a gentle check upon it. That is one thing. To work up emotion artificially is another.

On the question of silent intercessory prayer, John Austin Baker has an illuminating passage in his book, *The Foolishness of God*. This may not be the way for all, but for many, and in our day I think for an increasing number, it outlines the form their prayer may take. 'When we pray for others, we shall see that the most important requirement by far is inner calmness and tranquillity. We are not engaged in creating or producing anything, but in becoming aware of what is already the fact, namely that God is immediately and intimately present both to ourselves and to the one for whom we are praying. Our task is to hold the awareness of this fact in the still centre of our being, to unite our love for them with God's love, in the quiet but total confidence that he will use our love to help bring about the good in them which we both desire. In technical terms, therefore, intercession is a form of that kind of prayer known as "contemplation", with the special feature that here we contemplate not God in himself but God in his relationship of love to those whom we also love: and on the basis of our partnership with him we entrust our love into his hands to be used in harness with his own for their benefit.'

Before concluding, it will be right to turn our attention briefly to the question of miracle. We have already indicated that the very concept of prayer as we have defined it stands or falls on whether we allow or deny personality within the being of God. This thought is brought to its climax in the consideration of miracle.

It has been said earlier that many people would be prepared to defend prayer only at what might be called the psychological level. They would say, for example, that John's knowledge that Paul is praying for him in his sickness will be a comfort and strength, and an assurance that he is loved and cared for. Probably they would add that this knowledge might help John towards a new hope and courage, which in turn would be likely to react upon his bodily condition, so that the prayer offered would indeed assist his return to health. Certainly no Christian would be concerned to deny that this is one of the ways in which petitionary prayer acts. Nor, if he is wise, would he belittle its importance. But he will be bound to admit that to restrict the manner in which prayer operates to some such mode as this fails completely to do justice to the teaching of the New Testament, to our Lord's own teaching and example, to the witness of the early church, and indeed to the church's experience in every age, including our own. When our Lord said to blind Bartimaeus, 'Receive your sight', or when St Peter said to the cripple at the gate of the temple, 'In the Name of Jesus Christ of Nazareth stand up and walk' we are in the presence of a new creation; what takes place can in no sense be explained subjectively within the terms of raising a man's morale. We are in fact in the presence of miracle, which is to say, we are in the presence of the living God. And, as Christians, we know that one way in which miracle comes about is through God's response in answer to prayer. This is a matter for awe and wonder, and we may see it as part of that continual self-emptying of God of which the Word becoming flesh was the focal point and manifestation in space and time. Just as the father of a family 'empties himself' so that he does not make all the family decisions of his own unaided will but allows the wishes and requests of the children to be taken into account, so God has chosen to deal with his children. We may marvel at this and wonder how it can be, but the reason is surely not difficult to understand. Religion is not primarily concerned with right conduct but with relationships: 'henceforth I call you not servants but friends'; 'you have received the spirit of sonship whereby we cry "Abba Father" '. Right conduct in itself might lead only to egotism; but through prayer, and all that issues from it, relationships develop, fellowship and communion take on new depth. This is not, of course, to suggest that all answers to prayer are miracle; but the possibility of miracle can never be ruled out.

I think it ought to be added that belief in miracle does not mean that we believe that in answer to prayer God will suspend or change natural law on which the orderly ruling of the universe depends. If a child were to fall over a precipice the natural result would be for gravity to pull him to the ground. But if his father by an act of will stretches out his hand and grabs his son and pulls him back to safety, no one imagines gravity to have been suspended, but rather that a new force projected into the situation has had its way. So too when our Lord walked on the water we are not to suppose that the ordinary working of gravity was suspended, but that a new power, initiated by the divine will, interposed. The point is expressed as follows by Bishop Reichel (quoted in A. L. Worlledge's, *Prayer*): 'The intervention of the Divine will in answer to prayer, by simply directing the energies and powers of nature to a result which, if left undirected, they would not have arrived at, seems to me, on the most careful reflection, just as possible as that of which we see the results in every part of the globe at every moment—I mean the intervention of the human will not in the way of "suspending" or "superseding", but in the way of using the laws of nature by directing natural forces into certain channels.'

We note that the quotation begins with the words 'the intervention of the Divine will', and it is this which is always the essential element of miracle. In his booklet, *Our Understanding of Prayer,* the late Bishop I.T. Ramsey of Durham makes this same point, though rather more cautiously, in these words: 'Prayer undoubtedly supposes that it makes sense to speak of God's activity as directed to a particular point and as effecting something new in the universe. Does it? We all know how human effort can change the world and how by thought and skill we can create novelty on town and country. It is true that in our case this needs the intervention of our bodily organism. But if God is related to the whole universe in the way described earlier—on the analogy of ourselves to our bodies—this may still be a profitable reflection. In general terms we are only required to believe in principle that God can act within the texture of the universe, and certainly the Christian can have no fundamental difficulty with this concept. The Christian certainly cannot in principle exclude God's special activity in Christ from being effective in nature and human nature.'

Dr Farmer in his book *The World and God* lists three elements which he holds to be indispensable to miracle. 'First, there is an awareness of serious crisis or need or threat of disaster in the personal life, and of helplessness to deal with it adequately and victoriously through the exercise of ordinary, unaided powers. Second, there is a more or less conscious and explicit turning to God for assistance. Third, there is an awareness of an *ad hoc* response of God to the situation and to man's petitionary inadequacy in it, so that the crisis is met, the need satisfied, the danger averted in an event, or combination of events, which would not have taken place had not man so petitioned and God so acted.' Miracle then involves a special breaking in of God into the world, and in the sense in which Dr Farmer uses the term, this comes about in answer to man's prayer. We have no means of knowing ordinarily how often this may happen, or indeed whether when it has happened it is in answer to some specific prayer, for we do not forget that God knows our needs before we ask him. But for myself I believe—this is of faith, there can be no proof—that we are subject to divine or angelic protection much more frequently than we are likely to be aware.

I do not know how well known may be the following story of the beloved Bishop King, former Bishop of Lincoln. I tell it as far as I can remember as I received it from a younger member of the family. The Bishop was walking alone one night on one of the lonely fen roads outside Lincoln to visit a sick person to whom he had been summoned. When he arrived at the cottage he found no one had been ill, nor could anyone explain the message. The matter might well have ended there. But some years later a condemned murderer whom the Bishop had prepared for confirmation told him that he had sent the message, that he was waiting in the ditch to assault him and to rob him, but that to his surprise the Bishop had not come alone, but was flanked by a man on either side.

Even a Christian so aware of spiritual realities as Bishop King would have remained unconscious of divine protection apart from this unexpected sequel. And there may still be an element in the story unrevealed, some special prayer for the Bishop's safety. If we go strictly by Dr Farmer's definition, some such petition would seem necessary for the event to be called 'miracle'. But I would myself call the episode miraculous as it stands. We do not know just how God may have protected us, not just from bodily harm (probably not chiefly from that) but from spiritual dangers which might have quite overwhelmed us, nor to what extent other people's prayer may have been instrumental in this. No doubt the experience of visible angelic protection such as this story illustrates is of rare occurrence, but it is legitimate to wonder how much of what we generally call coincidence, or chance, or luck may not be due to a special Providence of God.

Naturally the question arises that if God can intervene and often does why does he not do so more often? What do we make of the car accidents, and the plane crashes, and the tragic shootings, and the whole field of disaster with which our papers are so largely filled, and the daily onset of fatal illness and sudden death? No definitive answer can ever be given to this question, though there are reflections that have to be made.

First, we shall recall that God did not intervene to prevent our Lord's own suffering and death on the cross, though he might have done so. Even after the victory of Gethsemane has been won, Jesus is conscious that there could still be a way of deliverance. 'Do you suppose', he says as the soldiers are about to lead him away, 'that I cannot appeal to my Father, who would at once send to my aid more than twelve legions of angels?' But that prayer was never made. The really breathtaking aspect of God's love is the Incarnation, its self-emptying and humiliation, leading to the anguish of Gethsemane and Calvary, where our Lord took on himself all the suffering man can experience, and more. The theoretical problem of suffering may remain, but in the power of the Spirit it is seen to be transcended and taken into the redemptive purpose of God. A Christian sees God working from within every suffering and tragedy, which in union with Christ becomes a redemptive experience for the world itself. Brother Edward, pioneer of the Village Evangelists, expresses this in one of his letters: 'I do seriously believe that all suffering patiently endured is linked with the one suffering in Christ in redeeming the world. I believe that if I can suffer bravely and put faith and courage and love into it, that suffering of mine will count towards the world's salvation. I believe that actually those who suffer in the Spirit are, under Christ, our greatest and most generous benefactors. They do more for us than the busiest who bustle about in service.'

A further reflection is that there must be in regard to God's special intervention a great economy of action, or the framework of order and discipline necessary for man's development would be overthrown. If God were to interfere in every situation in which we got ourselves into difficulty, all controlled and disciplined and planned life would be at an end. If fire were suddenly not to burn when children upset the oil stove, or the aircraft were not to fall when the mechanic had failed to tighten some vital nut, and if this same principle operated through every department of life, there could be no incentive to carefulness, responsibility, order, discipline. Moreover, every future event would be unpredictable, and planning impossible in any free human sense. It is because we are set in a framework of natural law which normally goes unhampered on its own majestic course, that life as a school and training ground for character can exist at all. If life were studded with miracles comparable to the stilling of the storm and the feeding of the five thousand, man in his present stage of moral development would be lost. When these things happen once in a way, as when God visited this planet in human form, they serve to reveal the autonomy of his creative power, and to awaken adoration and trust. When the Queen visits a school a week's holiday is given. The school can absorb that because there is only one queen, and she is not likely to return for a hundred years. No school could survive a monthly royal visit, and no economic system could survive a frequent multiplication of the loaves.

Yet, as a final consideration, are we sure we should wish for miracle even if we saw it as a possibility? Probably many people think of miracle as a reward to man's faith. We may forget it may equally be a concession to his weakness. The stilling of the storm is just such a case. Our Lord's primary will for the disciples was not that it should be calmed, but that they should have met it with untroubled hearts in serenity and trust. Hence he rebuked not merely the winds and the waves, but the disturbed and agitated men whose faith had failed. Those who have grasped the values and priorities of the kingdom will know that its deepest rewards belong where troubles, distresses, calamities, misfortunes—whatever form the storm may take—have been accepted and passed through lovingly and trustfully in God's saving grace. This does not mean that God's succour is not to be accepted in whatever way it is offered. It would indeed be highly presumptuous to assume that we know best the way of our deliverance. But the whole tenor of the New Testament is that deliverance shall normally be expected *through*—and not *from*—trial and affliction. The reward for the man who has built his house upon the rock of the gospel is not that it shall be protected against the batterings of nature, but that after the rains have fallen, and the floods have come, and winds have blown, it shall remain firm. In the words of Mother Julian, 'He said not "thou shalt not be tempested" but "thou shalt not be overcome".'

Chapter 2

APPROACH TO CONTEMPLATION

The first point which governs all that I shall have to say is that life must be taken and accepted as a whole, and prayer can never be separated from life, excepting for the purpose of analysis. Of course a good deal depends on how we define prayer. Some people speak of prayer as though to equate it with Christian living. They would say that caring for old people, or visiting the sick in hospital, this was their way of praying. If we choose to enlarge our definition of prayer in this way we must also allow it to include washing up, or gardening, or earning a living, or travelling to work, or doing the cross-word, or eating and drinking and sleeping. The whole range of life will be included. And we should indeed be on shaky grounds if we were to affirm that any one of these activities had in itself greater value in the sight of God than any other. For the value of any work is to be judged by the love which inspires it in response to God's calling to that particular work rather than in the nature of the work itself. In that great little spiritual classic, *The Practice of the Presence of God*, Brother Lawrence with true insight saw all perfection in such a simple act as picking a straw from the ground if only it could be done solely for the love of God. This action would be a purer form of prayer than the performance of some work beneficial to society in which the motivation was deficient in love. 'Though I give all my goods to feed the poor, though I give my body to be burned and have not love . . .'

Now whilst I am ready to go along with this view, which sees prayer as co-extensive with Christian living, and further to agree that in holding it some important principles are conserved—it makes impossible, for example, a false antithesis between secular and religious—yet clearly this will not be an acceptable view of prayer for the purpose of these chapters. For if I were to adopt it I should find myself writing on the whole range of

Christian life instead of on some specific activity within it. In these pages we shall regard prayer as the activity in which we are engaged when, alone or in the company of others, our hearts and minds and wills are occupied with God and him alone; and we shall regard the Christian's activity, whether religious so-called or secular so-called, as the overspill of prayer into daily life. In all life God is to be glorified, but the only way in which in fact this is likely to be so is by ensuring that we take regular times in which he is sought and he alone, in which every motive other than the glory of God is, as far as may be, excluded. God does not value our prayer time because it is in itself valuable above all other times, but because all other times are meant to be charged with the meaning of this particular time. John Dalrymple in *The Christian Affirmation* has well summarised our point in the thought, 'You are never likely to be able to pray everywhere all the time, unless you first learn to pray somewhere some of the time'.

But in so limiting prayer, we shall remember that it is never to be disengaged from the total offering of life. It is the possibility that this may happen and sometimes has happened, that has so often brought the subject of prayer into disrepute. And so we must stress as a thread running through all our thoughts that prayer can never be compartmentalised from life. Prayer and living will continually be acting and reacting on one another. Insofar as our daily work is not open to the impulse and direction of the Holy Spirit, to that extent will our prayer life be weakened. And conversely insofar as there is a holding back or want of openness in our prayer life, to that extent what we offer to God in our work will be enfeebled. If at any time there seems to be a dedication in our prayer life without a corresponding dedication in our work then that will be an appearance only. Our work will be the test of the reality of our prayer. Naturally it will take time for prayer to break through for the consecration of the whole of life. Ultimately each side of life will move towards perfection supported and encouraged by the other.

The second point which underlies all that we shall say is that only the Holy Spirit can teach us how to pray. That is so obvious that it is almost trite. We hear it again and again, and we meet it in all the books. Perhaps just for that reason we pay less attention than we should. We shall find help and direction from books and people. Yet finally prayer is the work of the Holy Spirit within us, and ultimately he alone is our teacher. The Spirit, says St Paul, comes to the aid of our weakness. We do not even know how we ought to pray 'but the Spirit himself makes intercession for us with groanings that cannot be uttered'. Perhaps here we come near to a definition of contemplative prayer. 'Groanings which cannot be uttered', or as the *R.S.V.* puts it, 'sighs too deep for words'—or as my commentary paraphrases, 'inexpressible longings which God alone understands'. Contemplation is indeed a gift, a gift of the Spirit, and only the Spirit can take us to it and lead us in it. It should be awaited rather than sought, and if sought it should be gently sought in patience abiding God's time rather than our own. The Spirit moves where he wills, and whether it be in vocal prayer, in tongues, or in the silence of contemplation only he can teach us how to pray.

Many years ago when I was about 24, I remember going for a walk with Father Wigram who at that time was Superior of the Cowley Fathers at St Edward's House. Father Wigram was a man of considerable spiritual stature as those who knew him will recall. Bede Frost's book, *The Art of Mental Prayer*, had recently been published and was enjoying a good deal of popularity. At the heart of the book is described the various methods of meditative prayer: the Oratorian, the Carmelite, the Ignation, the Franciscan, and others. I should be unable to say much about them now, but I had read the book at the time and no doubt I said a good deal. We were nearing the end of our walk when I turned to Father Wigram and said, 'And Father, how do *you* pray?' A few moments silence and then he said, 'Well I usually kneel down and hope for the best'. It was a rebuke I well deserved, not perhaps intended as such. The saints have a way of making devastating remarks with artless simplicity. To kneel down and hope for the best is good advice if we see hope as a theological virtue (with faith and charity), the confident expectation that God the Holy Spirit will complete within us the good work which he has begun. And every period of prayer is a taking forward of this process. It has taken me many years to learn to kneel down and hope for the best. Let us not forget the place of freedom and simplicity in prayer.

But to say that is not to imply that prayer like everything else does not have its own technique. And this brings me to my third point. I hope you will not be bothered if I use this word 'technique' in relation to prayer. The fact that it can be misused should not prevent us capturing its proper use. People sometimes say, and especially is it being said in these days in which gurus and maharishis are being increasingly sought out in the western world, that prayer is some form of technique. That is quite wrong, at least so far as Christian prayer is concerned, and it needs to be contradicted. But to affirm the place of technique within the life of prayer is quite another matter and indeed we should be foolish to neglect it. The end of prayer is encounter, encounter with the living God—communion or fellowship we may equally call it—and technique must always be subordinate to encounter. As I write these words, I hope to make encounter, I hope that my spirit may commune with my readers' spirits, and to that end I must use a technique, in this case that of writing words in the English tongue. Two years ago I was asked to give a talk to some of the Sisters in a Convent in France. The nuns knew little English and I knew less French, and since the technique was poor the encounter was spoiled. Perhaps we shall want to say it is not quite the same when we speak to God. God looks upon the heart and not on the lips, and outward forms, of which language is one and posture is another, become matters of indifference. So I think we must say that technique is important from *our* point of view and not from God's. Have you ever watched yourself or your friend speaking on the telephone? We nod our head up and down or we shake it from side to side, perhaps we clinch a point by making a gesture with our free arm, all of which is very foolish since the one we are speaking to cannot see us, but reasonable and even sensible if it enables us to communicate better. If then technique helps in prayer we should be foolish to despise it. One of the points we shall come to later is the importance of posture in silent prayer, and of the correlation between tension and relaxation in different parts of the body. More attention is paid to this in the non-Christian East than in the West. The truth is that you can approach a matter of this sort in two ways. Take for example the relationship of sleep to posture. Supposing you are out for a picnic and sitting on the grass and you fall asleep. Your body will at once take up a posture suited to sleep, a horizontal position on the ground. But you could start from the other end and say, 'Now that I want to go to sleep I shall first lie down on the ground, and then, given the desire for sleep, it will soon overtake me'. You have the same choice in prayer. In contemplative prayer the body will tend to assume the posture best suited to that state. By taking up the posture most suited for prayer, then, given the desire and intention to pray, the end we are looking for—prayer itself—will be brought about. Now to many people that sounds horribly artificial and mechanical in relationship to prayer. Yet every night in regard to sleep, we first take the correct posture and then let sleep overtake us—and there is no difference in principle between the two. Of course only the Holy Spirit can enable us to pray. But that should not prevent us assuming a posture which will assist his action in us. There are dangers, it is true, lest we mistake outward form for inner reality. But if we are alert, we need have no fear.

Then, as my next point, I want us to keep to the fore the idea of prayer as an offering. This is especially true in praise and thanksgiving, and in our waiting upon God in silence. The psalmist you will remember says, 'I will offer unto God the sacrifice of thanksgiving and will call upon the name of the Lord.' The same thought is given Christian content by the writer of the Epistle to the Hebrews where we read, 'Through Jesus let us continually offer up to God the sacrifice of praise, that is the tribute of the lips which acknowledge his name'. Our offering in prayer is to be linked with the offering of Jesus, in virtue of which we are reconciled to God, and so may offer ourselves as sons to their father. We are enabled to make this offering, not of ourselves, but through the prevenient action of the Holy Spirit. Yet the offering *is* ours, for God does not override our freedom—it is ours as a response to grace, a response gladly and freely given. And since this offering is made through Jesus, we shall be encouraged in remembering it cannot be made alone, but is a part of the total offering of his mystical body the Church.

If we are able to see prayer quite simply in this way as an offering, one important consequence will follow. We shall be relieved of all desire to make prayer 'successful', whatever that may mean. And that will save us from discouragement which is perhaps the commonest reason why people do not persevere with their prayer life. What we are doing in silent prayer often appears to us at the time to be futile and, since this is an appearance only, one of the soundest pieces of advice for anyone who is finding prayer difficult, is that it is never to be judged by how it seems to be at the time but by its later fruits. If we can see prayer quite simply as an offering, we need not be bothered by questions which at the time may arise in our minds. 'Is this prayer helping me or anyone else? Is it strengthening?' Despise the thought. Offerings were never meant to help or strengthen, they are meant simply to be offered. 'Is this prayer helping my troubled mind and emotions?' Ignore it. Offerings are not meant to do that. They are meant to be offered. We leave our offerings confidently and lovingly in God's hands. We do not demand that this or that may come of them. If we can bring this pattern of thought into our prayers they will be delivered from one great enemy of prayer—subjectivity—those sideways glances at ourselves to see how we are getting along, and our lives will in fact be increasingly rooted and grounded in God. We have already reflected how prayer and activity react on one another, and the same idea of offering of course applies to our daily work. The important thing about our work is not that it is a success as we generally understand the word, but that it is generously and lovingly offered, and it may help to return to that thought from time to time. But I believe we are likely to see this dimension in our work only if we are learning to see it in our prayers.

Offerings, as we know, are liable to go wrong. A month or so ago a family in India sent me a gift of sweets. It came out of a background of poverty we should find hard to imagine in the Western world, and when the parcel reached me the food was spoilt and had to be thrown away. But the value of the offering, lying not in the gift but in the love which prompted it, remains unchanged. So we may know that our prayers, though of little worth, yet are accepted for love's sake. These are very simple thoughts, but we cannot be too simple before God. Keep them in mind and you will be helped by them.

Yet it worries some people when one speaks of prayer as an offering. They ask if it does not make God like an Eastern potentate who takes delight in the homage of his subjects. That is a false picture and quite an arbitrary one. For God is not to be compared to an Oriental monarch but to a father, a father who takes delight in his child's offering, not because his ego is thereby inflated, but because in the total action the relationship between father and son is being enlarged, and in this progression the father rightly delights. Father Benson of Cowley has written 'God appointed prayer . . . not because he had any delight in our formal homage but because he desired, by forming in us the habit of prayer, to draw us to look to himself the fountain of all good.' As John Macquarrie has said in his *Paths of Spirituality* 'The glorification of God and the sanctification of man are not competing motives in worship.' And he quotes St Irenaeus as presenting in a few words the paradox which is always present in the situation of worship: 'The glory of God is a living man; and the life of man consists in beholding God'.

Now we are to consider a simple level of contemplative prayer, or as I shall sometimes refer to it, the prayer of silence. In doing this I do not wish to suggest that vocal prayer such as, for example, the saying of the offices may not also be an exercise in contemplation. It may well be, for example, that in the saying of the psalms we are drawn beyond the words to the very heart of prayer. Our attention is now not so much to the words as to God himself. Father Augustine Baker of the seventeenth century, whose book *Holy Wisdom* is a classic of spiritual direction, writes of vocal prayer that it 'were ordained to this end, to supply and furnish the soul that needs with good matter . . . by which it may be united to God'. The words of the office then become the framework of our prayer, and are there to support us when we need them. May I give you a simple illustration? As I looked out of my window the other day, I saw a large and rather old pheasant on the lawn. It ran gaily along the ground, then took a short flight, and then being tired returned to the earth again; then after a little more running another flight and so on. It occurred to me that that can be rather like the saying of the offices. We move steadily along from verse to verse of the psalms, and then there may be a short period, as it were, on the wing when the words though still recited recede into the background, and somehow we are taken beyond them and held for a few moments in that stillness which is God. And then—and this too is the point—just as our pheasant had the good solid earth to return to and support him as he moved forward again, so we have the words of the office to return to and be our support. The bird could not just fall into a void, and in the same way the words of the office prevent us falling back into the distracting and discordant imagery which often holds our minds. We might well have approached the office from another angle. Indeed it would have been more natural to do so. I have not done so because I have wanted to show how the office might be a way in to contemplative prayer, little bursts of it as the bird makes little bursts of flight. But before the office does this for us, the repetition of its words with due attention paid to them as the Spirit empowers us, can be a tremendous help in enabling us to collect our minds, and to leave behind the distractions and concerns and perplexities of life which so often scatter our mental and spiritual energy. That is primary for all of us. I have not mentioned it first only because it is not primary for our present task.

It will help to make what I am saying more clear if you will picture to yourselves three parallel horizontal lines. The middle line stands for the words of the office. The line below it stands for the distracting occupations of daily living, and the words of the office are the agent of the Spirit continually to draw our minds above these things. The top line stands for contemplative prayer, and there will be times when the Spirit takes us beyond the words into the stillness which is God. Note that we are taken, we do not make the leap ourselves, it just happens as we go on our way. Yet all the time the words remain to support us as we may need them.

Yet we have to be realistic and say that for one reason or another the daily office has largely dropped out of the worshipping life of the Church, and that the opportunities which were open to people of an older generation are by and large not open today. But what I have said is not wasted, because the same underlying principles apply to another form of vocal prayer to which it seems many are called today, and which too can be a way in to contemplative silence. Many Christian people, though they probably will not speak of it unless it be to one or two like minded friends, use some sort of vocal prayer frequently repeated such as the Jesus Prayer, which was made known to the Western world largely through *The Way of a Pilgrim,* which made its first appearance in English about forty years ago. Perhaps this is the best introduction to the prayer, as we there meet it kindled in a human heart.* As many of you will know, the full form of the Jesus Prayer is, 'Lord Jesus Christ, Son of the Living God, have mercy on me a sinner'. But it has various shorter forms, and can be reduced to the oft repeated single word, 'Jesus'. It is not of course just an exercise of the lips. Far from it! The heart and mind will be in a very simple way, and not in any sort of strained way, enfolded in what is being said. I should only want to commend this prayer to those who have a special drawing to it. But I think that some form of repetitive vocal prayer (with cautions against indiscriminate use which we shall come to later) is likely to be a help to many who have not yet found that way. The psalms, of course, supply an inexhaustible treasury. 'Praise the Lord O my soul, and all that is within me praise his holy name'; 'Make me a clean heart O God and renew a right spirit within me'; 'Be still and know that I am God'. Equally, we could take something longer, such as a psalm known by heart, or a collect, or verses of a hymn. Whatever it is thus becomes to us *our* office, and like the offices of the Church not only does it preserve us from a dissipation of our energies (think again if you will of the three parallel lines), but it is a launching pad for the silent prayer of the heart. It has to be used with discretion and there can be danger of a

*For an excellent description of this way, I also recommend the chapter, 'The Prayer of the Name', in the S.P.C.K. publication *Prayer* written by Abhishiktananda, a French Benedictine monk who made his home in India.

C

zeal which outruns wisdom. It is always good if we can turn to some experienced person with whom we can discuss these things. In using such prayers the great thing is to mean 'God', and to go on meaning God whether the actual words at any particular moment seem to have meaning for us or not. When the words fade away into the background, we can still mean God beyond the words.

But some people ask of this form of prayer 'Is not this vain repetition, and are we not warned against that?' The answer must be that it is certainly repetition, but it is not necessarily vain. The hammering of a nail can be vain repetition if it moves not a fraction of an inch; but if each blow takes it, even minutely, nearer its object the work is no longer vain. So too, if every repetition of our prayer helps to unite us, however little, more closely with God, who is the end of all prayer, then the prayer is profitable and not vain. It is right to go gently with this form of prayer, keeping it within our means, and using it for perhaps not more than ten minutes at a time at first; we can then see how we are taken on from there. The 'Jesus Prayer' itself is rather special, though by no means exclusive, to the Orthodox Church, so that it is in their classical collection of spiritual writings, the *Philokalia* that we shall expect to find advice. And here we find not once, but a number of times, stress being laid on what is called 'drawing the mind through the heart'—a phrase that will apply equally whether we use the Jesus Prayer or some other form of words. We are helped to do this if we look down mentally towards the heart, and after a time the prayer will become for short periods, as it were, lodged in the heart, and it will go on for a while of its own accord. In a beautiful little book *On the Invocation of the Name of Jesus* published by the Fellowship of St Alban and St Sergius, a lovely likeness has been drawn to this form of prayer and the flight of a bird, it may be that of an eagle. Through the steady measured rhythmic beating of her wings the great bird ascends higher and higher into the upper reaches of the air. Then the time comes when the wings are spread and still, as she glides in graceful flight. After a while when height has been lost, the motion of the wings begins again. So whatever form our prayer may take the actual repetition of the words will ebb and flow; yet, for those who are practised in it, it is ever carried in the heart. What matters in life beyond all else is that the heart and mind of man be stayed on God—whether we call it habitual recollection or prayer without ceasing is of no account—and in so far and only in so far as repetitive prayer assists that end is it to be cherished and practised. We ought, however, to sound a warning because this form of prayer used indiscriminately can stir the unconscious levels of the mind beyond our immediate capacity to deal with them. It has been powerfully and cogently said that 'the pain of deepening self knowledge is to be kept not at a bearable minimum, nor at an intolerable maximum, but at a creative optimum'. Interpret that packed sentence in relationship to food, and then transfer it to the realm of prayer. In eating there is a creative optimum, the amount which best suits us for our daily work. Below this is a bearable minimum, but this leaves us too weak adequately to meet life's demands. And above it is an intolerable maximum which overtaxes the digestion and provides the body with more than it can hope to assimilate. So too at every stage there is a right proportion in prayer. However, with that caution, let it be said that the general need is to stimulate and encourage the timid rather than to restrain the confident. Some of you will have known this way of prayer for a long while. To others it may be new. To you I would say that if your heart warms to what I say, and you feel a desire for this way, then take that as the Spirit's leading and test it for a while. But if what I say makes no appeal, then accept it that this is not your way, at least for the present. And in any case, many are taken on to silent contemplation without this type of vocalisation being a stage of their prayer life.

Yet we are still only on the threshold of our subject. What I have been describing is perhaps best seen as a way in to contemplative prayer. Often it forms a bridge on from a type of prayer of which we do not hear very much today though it was widely practiced in the past, I mean the prayer of meditation. We shall not stay long here but it is worth saying a few words. Meditation, as Christians use that word (Eastern religions use it in a different sense), means basically taking some passage such as a story from the Bible, reading it, examining it, pondering upon it, considering how it affects my life and my relationship with others, and forming some resolution pertaining to the theme. At the end there will be some form of free prayer. The Bible Reading Fellowship is one among many schemes for those who use this way. Many of us have thus been launched on our prayer life, and if we find this pattern fruitful we should continue with it. Let me add that the way of contemplation does not mean that there will no longer be a place for the meditative hearing or reading of the scriptures, or of other books relating to the faith. What it does mean is that we shall find that these occupations now do no more than touch the fringe of what we might call our real prayer.

For there comes a time in the life of many people when this way of meditation is no longer satisfying. Even more than that, it becomes very difficult if not practically impossible for them to use it in their prayer time. If this development is accompanied by a deep longing for God, if we find ourselves just wanting him and him alone, then we may take this as an indication that the Holy Spirit is leading us on to contemplative prayer, and we must be content to leave discursive meditation behind and yield to the impress of the Spirit. 'Like as the hart desireth the water brooks, so longeth my soul after thee O God'; 'When I awake after thy likeness I shall be satisfied'. Settled or returning aspirations such as these may be taken as sure signs of the contemplative call. At the same time everyday things are likely to become less satisfying than before. There may perhaps be some withdrawal, though in the end we shall be likely to come back to all the good things of God's creation, but in a different way—they will now be caught up in the love of God and become the overflow of prayer into daily life. I am describing what is a well trodden path in the pilgrimage of the spirit. St John-of-the-Cross is the authority usually referred to, and he gives the signs three times in his writings. Many of you will recognise this as a stage in your own life, perhaps many years ago. But just as when one is motoring and has no map and moves into unexpected country, one is worried lest one has lost the way, so some people, when the old ways of prayer are no longer possible, become worried and discouraged, and because the silent ways in which they are now drawn involve such simplifications of memory and mind and will, they may begin to ask whether they are now really praying at all. Very possibly they now try to turn back to the old way, and finding it fruitless they are tempted to give up altogether. This is where knowledge of the well worn paths of the Spirit may reinforce our faith and enable us to persevere. What is happening is neatly summarised in this short definition of Father Stanton's, which distinguishes meditation from contemplation: 'Meditation is a detachment from the things of the world in order to attend to the things of God. Contemplation is a detachment from the things of God in order to attend to God himself.'

Before we go further we ought to make it clear that this silence of which we are speaking is not the silence of blankness or idleness which could never be a part of the Holy Spirit's calling. I think we might describe it under two images. You could think of a sentry on duty and describe the silence as one of alertness or awareness. Or you could think of two people who deeply love one another, and describe it as a silence of understanding and perception and harmony. We all know how different silences can be. There can be an idle silence or an embarrassed silence, and better than either is conversation in which we try to develop an awareness of one another's needs and interests. But that is only a stage, just as discursive meditation is only a stage, and sooner or later there will be a break-through, and long periods can now pass, perhaps before the fire of a winter's evening, when each is supported by the silent presence of the other, conversation being now superfluous, or at least being allowed to come and go quite freely as it will. That is the picture of contemplative silence.

In approaching contemplative prayer in this way, I do not want the inference to be made that people nowadays are generally drawn to contemplation through the earlier discipline of meditation. Historically speaking this is no doubt true, But formal meditation is much less taught and practised today and the contemplative call is likely to be a direct one. Any who find within their hearts an answering cry to St Augustine's great words, 'Thou hast made us for thyself and the heart of man is restless till it finds its rest in thee', and who are ready in the grace of God to face the testing experiences of the way, should go forward, nothing doubting, in the path in which the Spirit is now calling.

Chapter 3

CONTEMPLATION AND HEALING

In pursuit of our study of contemplation I now want to turn to a book which has very much come into its own in our day, *The Cloud of Unknowing,* a work belonging to the fourteenth century. It is available in several editions, ancient and modern, but if you wish to buy a copy I recommend the Penguin edition in modern speech. In a valuable introduction, Clifton Wolters writes of the author as a man of a 'well-stored and scholarly mind, with a flair for expressing complexities simply; there was more than a streak of the poet in him, and at the same time a saving sense of humour and proportion. Probably most people would feel that they would like to know him, and some at least might wish they could have his guidance today.' This indeed is what we shall now seek.

The Cloud was written to a young disciple who had, no doubt, appealed to the author for training in prayer. Through him it is addressed to a larger public, and yet by no means to everybody nor yet to every devout Christian, but only to those who by the inner working of the Spirit God has disposed towards contemplation. We have already examined what it is which constitutes that call.

We may start with chapter 3. 'Lift up your heart to God with humble love; and mean God and not what you get out of him.' Here at the very beginning we are reminded of a suggestion made earlier, that we should try to see prayer as an offering. Now it must be that a part of the offering is the offering of time. And on this we must be clear from the start. It is almost too obvious to say that there can be no prayer unless there is time given for prayer. I am not suggesting that this is easy in an ordinary household, but I do believe it would have to be an extraordinary household for it to be impossible. But once the time is set aside and adhered to, more than half the battle is won. The fact is that prayer is so much like hard work that most of us find very ordinary things like writing a letter or making a phone call take on an exaggerated importance when the prayer time comes round. But to continue: '. . . hate to think of anything but God himself so that nothing occupies your mind or will but only God. Try to forget all created things . . . Let them go and pay no attention to them . . . Do not give up but work away . . . When you first begin you find only darkness and a cloud of unknowing . . . Reconcile yourself to wait in this darkness as long as is necessary, but go on longing after him you love . . .'; and then later 'strike that thick cloud of unknowing with the sharp dart of longing love and on no account think of giving up.'

Let us stop here for a moment. We have taken up our position for prayer, and we have called upon the Holy Spirit explicitly or in the silent desire of the heart, and we are now to let everything go, our thoughts, our imaginations, our memories, everything excepting this one thing which remains—and here is a phrase which keeps recurring in *The Cloud*, 'a naked intention directed towards God and him alone'. The one thing necessary, the author says, is to 'mean God who created you, and bought you and graciously called you to this state of life'. But how can we in practice retain this intention? We shall almost certainly need some simple thought as a focal point for the mind, and so the author allows us a word such as 'God' or 'love' or some other word given to us. This word he says is to be 'fixed fast to the heart' (and at once we note the likeness to the *Philokalia* in its references to 'drawing the mind through the heart') 'so that' our writer continues 'it is always there come what may. It will be your shield and spear in peace and war alike.' There is no need for the word to be framed with the lips (this may or may not help, whether it is said aloud or under the breath). Best of all, when we are ready, it can be seen mentally in the heart. But we should not feel bound to any word. A word is given for our help if we need it. In chapter 39, the author writes 'if God leads you to certain words my advice is not to let them go, that is, if you are using words at all in your prayer.' Ultimately they will tend to slip away, and we shall be left simply looking down into the heart and meaning God, and continuing to mean him and him alone. What the author insists on in regard to words, if we use them, is that they shall be taken whole, and not be analysed. We take perhaps the word 'God', but we must resist the temptation to reflect on him at this time. This is not the time for considering discursively his love and goodness, nor his reconciling work in our Lord's passion. Indeed there will be a time for this but not now. This is the time for knowing God and loving him, not for reflecting upon him. This is the time—inevitably we come back to the phrase—for 'reaching out with a naked intent of the will towards God'. And let us not forget, mentally we are to look downwards and see him in our hearts.

The Cloud does not say much about posture. The author tells us that the body will of its own accord tend to take up the position most suited to prayer. He writes in chapter 61, 'For when a soul is determined to engage in this work, then, at the same time (and the contemplative does not notice it) his body which perhaps before he began tended to stoop because this was easier, now through the Spirit holds itself upright, and follows physically what has been done spiritually. All very fitting!' Whether kneeling, sitting or standing, the back inevitably tends to straighten out in this prayer, as all who practise it will know. We must return to this question, but let me just say now that older people, and perhaps many younger people, too, may well find that sitting erect in an upright chair is the best position. There are some to whom sitting suggests a want of reverence. But we need not feel like that. Perhaps the author used it himself. We know that it was the favourite posture of Richard Rolle, one of the great English mystics of the period of *The Cloud*. 'Sitting', he would say—I quote from Father Verrier Elwyn's book *Richard Rolle*—'I am most at rest and my heart most upward. I have loved to sit for thus I loved God more and I remained longer within the comfort of love than if I were walking or standing or kneeling.' And we may perhaps recall that it was while the Church was seated that the Holy Spirit first descended upon it at Pentecost.

Described thus, prayer sounds easy enough, and in fact in chapter 3 of *The Cloud* the author does make that very claim, that it is the easiest work of all when a soul is helped by grace and has a conscious longing for prayer. No doubt there is a real sense in which that is true. You may remember the Old Testament story of Jacob, how he toiled for Laban for seven years that he might win Rachel's hand. From what we know of Laban, Jacob's work involved a good deal of sweat and tears. And yet we read that for the love he bore to Rachel they seemed to him but a few days. It was love which rendered the work easy, and that too is true of our work of prayer. But the author is at no pains to conceal the cost which is involved. In chapter 26 he writes, 'It is hard work . . . very hard work indeed . . .' It is likely to be no accident that he refers to his prayer as work, for so indeed it is. Prayer has about it the two qualities which you usually expect to find in work. It is on the one hand costly to the one who works, and on the other beneficial to the community which includes the worker himself. And if we are called to contemplative prayer and are to respond to the Spirit's call, we must face the fact that this will call for the sacrifice of time, for courage to persevere, for patience to endure the pain of deepening self knowledge, for fortitude in times of temptation, for faith when the way is obscure, and for the love which is ready to make every new surrender as the Spirit calls. That is one side of the work, the side which is costly to the giver, and we may well ask, who is sufficient for these things? But there is too the other side, the social side, the side which serves the community, and how can we serve the community better than by engaging in this work of healing and reconciliation, of making men whole within the Body of Christ? For that is what this work effects. It has been well said that contemplatives war against the real enemy, and ultimately against the only enemy; for whereas in the world we are up against effects, contemplatives are face to face with causes, with the ultimate truths which lie behind the visible.

I expect some of you remember the story of Robert Hugh Benson in which he tells of a lonely chapel in which a nun is praying. To this chapel there comes one whom we might call a visionary or a sensitive, someone who possesses unusually perceptive psychic sensibility. To the ordinary observer nothing is happening in that chapel. Simply a nun is praying. But to the visionary the unseen world reveals its secrets. Teilhard de Chardin re-tells the story. 'All at once he [the visionary] sees the whole world bound up and moving and organising itself around this out of the way spot, in tune with the intensity and inflection of that puny, praying figure. The convent chapel has become the axis about which the earth revolves. The contemplative sensitised and animated all things because she believed; and her faith was operative because her very pure soul placed her near to God.' 'This piece of fiction', de Chardin adds, 'is an admirable parable', and he continues that 'if we could see the light invisible as we could see the clouds or lightning or rays of the sun, a pure soul would seem as active in this world by virtue of its sheer purity, as the snowy summits whose impassable peaks breathe in continually for us the roving power of the high atmosphere.'

The author of *The Cloud* does not hesitate to make this sort of claim for his work on what we might call the community side. His words are:

'All saints and angels rejoice over it and hasten to help it on with all their might . . . Moreover the whole of mankind is wonderfully helped by what you are doing in ways you do not understand. Yes, the very souls in purgatory find their pain eased by virtue of your work . . . and in no better way can you be made clean or virtuous than by attending to this.'

How little we know of our true helpers! Father Martin Thornton observes in *Christian Proficiency*: 'I rather feel that some of us are in for a shock when in the Church expectant we discover the real perspective for world redemption; the achievement of the Prime Minister and the Foreign Secretary may look pretty small compared with the influence wrought by little Miss Perkins of Honeysuckle Cottage.' And do we realise that as we grow older, and the vigour of body and mind begin to decline, this is the work which the Holy Spirit desires to entrust increasingly to the faithful, the work which the author of *The Cloud* does not hesitate to describe as the most far reaching and deepest work of all?

We must now turn to the second cloud—for, as our author says, there are two clouds, not one—the cloud of forgetting. We meet it first in chapter 5, and I will quote what is said there: 'Just as this cloud of unknowing is as it were above you, between you and God, so you must also put a cloud of forgetting between you and all creation . . . Everything must be hidden under this cloud of forgetting . . . Indeed, if we may say so reverently, when we are engaged on this work it profits little or nothing to think even of God's kindness or worth, or of our Lady, or of the saints or angels, or of the joys of heaven . . . it may be good sometimes to think particularly about God's kindness and worth . . . yet in the work before us it must be put down and covered with the cloud of forgetting.' The author allows no exception. He goes on to insist that everything must be put down under this cloud. We have already seen that any theological speculation is forbidden at this time. Equally forbidden are all memories and imaginations, recollection of happy occasions and beautiful things, anxious thoughts and painful memories which may so often, even against our will, disturb and trouble us, memories of past sins of which we have perhaps long since repented and received forgiveness—all these things and all else are to be pressed down under the cloud of forgetting. This is not for the destruction of imagination and memory—they will function ordinarily at other times—but in and through this prayer there will be a growing purification of these faculties and a detachment from them, so that in course of time we may become their master instead of being their servant as is so often now the case. The near compulsive grip which these things may have upon us in certain areas of our lives will be broken, and in the exercise of this prayer the Spirit will take us on into an ever growing freedom.

As the book goes on, the author becomes yet more insistent on this cloud of forgetting. What perhaps is likely to cause special trouble is memories of past sins. Yet we are to take courage, and to be in no way disheartened by this. Let me quote the whole of chapter 31. It is only thirteen lines. 'When you have done all you can to make the proper amendment laid down by Holy Church then get to work quick sharp. If memories of your past actions keep coming between you and God, or any new thought or sinful impulse, you are resolutely to step over them, because of your deep love for God; you must trample them down under foot. Try to cover them with the thick cloud of forgetting as though they had never been committed by you or anyone else. And indeed as often as they come up push them down. And if it is really hard work you can use every dodge, scheme, and spiritual strategem you can find to put them away. These arts are better learnt from God by experience than from any human teacher.'

Are we perhaps alarmed by the vigour of these words? Do they perhaps suggest 'repression' as that word is used in the language of psychology? I am not thinking of suppression of thought which occurs every time we choose to think of one thing rather than another. Thus when the bell goes the schoolboy suppresses the thought of Latin that he may now think of mathematics. Repression as I use the word stands for a compulsory and involuntary forgetting of experience or memories which the mind has found too painful to retain in conscious thought. A mark of true repression is that the memory cannot be recalled at will however hard the person may try. That does not mean it is out of harm's way. This is certainly no case of 'out of sight, out of mind', for it can send up all sorts of disguised fears and compulsions to the conscious mind, and many people suffer physical disability, sickness, paralysis, blindness, through fears and conflicts which remain repressed. 'You mean doctor I have a boil in my unconscious', seemed to me when I read it to be a nicely graphic description of a repression. Psychologically speaking, *suppression* is harmless, *repression* is dangerous. It is convenient to have the two words, standing as they do for different concepts. Yet they cannot be kept entirely apart, for repression could follow suppression if the suppression were persistent, and the thought suppressed highly emotionally charged.

I think from what the author of *The Cloud* writes in the chapter following the one I have just quoted, which we shall come to later, that he would have been fully alert to the danger of repression, psychologically understood. The great spiritual directors were good psychologists, though necessarily, since they lived in a bygone age, their knowledge of that science was intuitive rather than analytical. I have been interested to read in Dr Morton Kelsey's book *Healing and Christianity* how he, the author, asked Jung what was the nearest method of counselling to Jung's own method. He was expecting Jung to name some psychological school or other, but instead he replied, 'The classical direction of conscience of the 19th century in France'. The directors of this period would have drawn freely on those before them. Names such as St Francis de Sâles, Fénelon, de Caussade and others come to mind.

Before we go further, let us distinguish between different types of memories. There are first what I shall call the emotionally neutral class, and these are by far the greater number. What is it we have done today? Well, if you think back, we got out of bed, we dressed and washed, we had our breakfast, we walked to our work, and so on. All such memories belong to the emotionally neutral class, and if they recur during prayer they should not cause trouble. They are not difficult to ignore. Then there are other thoughts which are emotionally evocative but pleasantly and not disturbingly so. Such might be the memory of beautiful scenery, great art or music, friendship and so on. These too are to be put down at the time of contemplative prayer, and it is not likely that any problem will arise. More difficult is it to put away in time of prayer the memory of some work in which the mind has been deeply engrossed, some business problem, some talk we are preparing, some difficult letter perhaps. However, in none of these cases is there danger of repression as we are using that word. But there are other thoughts which will fit into none of these classes, thoughts which for one reason or another are highly emotionally charged, due perhaps to some repressed or partially repressed painful or traumatic experience, forgotten or largely forgotten, reaching back perhaps to early childhood, or some persistent fear, irrational it may be, taking on the strength of a phobia which we are largely powerless to control. Morbid guilt, overwhelming grief, deep seated inner resentment, wounded pride, jealousy, a sense of inferiority, scrupulosity, compulsive or near compulsive aggressions—these are the kinds of disorders (they may be disguised as they appear in consciousness) which are likely to cause trouble. But take courage. In our prayer they are finding their healing.

The author, we have noted, has said that everything is to be pressed down under a cloud of forgetting, but significantly he immediately goes on to say how memories may be dealt with when they do arise. And clearly he is here, as everywhere else, speaking from his own experience.

In clarification of this seeming contradiction, allow me, if you will, a simple illustration. Suppose you take your ten-year-old son to church. And since he has a tiresome cough you tell him not to cough during the sermon. At once you realise that that piece of advice standing alone will not do. Yet it has value because it gives him something to aim at. Without it he might cough freely and quite unnecessarily. But at once you will go on and say, 'But if you must cough'—well I don't know how you would go on! Perhaps we should say, 'Cough into your handkerchief and the noise will be muffled'. It is a very simple illustration, but it is the sort of advice the author is giving. He is telling us not to admit memories and imaginations in prayer, and this is valuable because it sets our sights upon God and upon him alone, and upon the word we are to keep before us to focus our attention. Without that advice we should be lost from the start. However much this boy of ours may have to cough in church it is essential he gets his priorities right and aims at self-control. If he does not do that it will be disastrous for all concerned, and better that church attendance had never been attempted. Equally, if we do not get our priorities right in prayer, which in the teaching of *The Cloud* is 'to reach out with a naked intent of the will towards God' so that nothing occupies our mind or will but only God himself—if we do not get this firmly implanted in our mind, then we shall find ourselves given over to the memories and distractions which crowd in, and our prayer time will be disastrous, a day dream rather than a prayer, and it would have been better if it had not been attempted. But once our sights have been truly set on God, with the desire and intention that in God's grace this shall remain so, we need not fear the memories and distractions which come into the imagination. What now becomes necessary is that we do not attend to them. Later I want us to see that these very things are in fact for our purification and our healing, so long as we are content simply to let them be, in no way voluntarily attending to them, but looking over their shoulder as it were to God.

In that phrase, 'looking over their shoulder', I have anticipated *The*

Cloud. For this is just what the author tells us to do. In the chapter following the one I quoted just now, he says, 'Do everything you can to act as if you did not know that these thoughts were strongly pushing in between you and God. Try to look over their shoulder seeking something else which is God shrouded in the cloud of unknowing.' So then we are to keep looking towards God, to be ready to suffer these thoughts if need be, 'to let them float' to use the words of popular psychology, but not to attend to them. We neither run away from them nor do we encourage them, we simply look to God in the midst of them.

I use the word 'simply', but I do not mean to imply by this that it will be easy. It is not for nothing that the author calls his prayer hard work, and there are likely to be days when the going is tough. Please do not think that I am suggesting a sinecure for your retirement and old age. What I am describing will call for quite as much resolution in the realm of the spirit as climbing a mountain in that of the body. This work is for men, not for canaries. How about this quotation from John Edward Southall, a Quaker of several generations ago? He is telling of an early experience of silence before God. It had been suggested to him by a friend that he should learn to be still in God's presence. This he thought would surely be an easy matter. But not at all. He writes that he had no sooner begun 'than a perfect pandemonium of voices reached my ears, a thousand clamouring notes from without and within, until I could hear nothing but their noise and din. Never before did there seem so many things to be done, to be said, to be thought, and in every direction I was pushed and pulled and greeted with noisy acclamations of unspeakable unrest. It seemed necessary for me to listen to some of them but God said "Be still and know that I am God". As I listened and slowly learnt to obey and shut my ears to every sound, I found after a while that when the other voices ceased, or I ceased to hear them, there was a still small voice in the depth of my being that began to speak with an inexpressible tenderness, power and comfort.' The writer is speaking of an early venture into silence, no doubt at a time when his daily life was marked by all sorts of distracting and dissipating thoughts, and we may believe that as the spirit of recollection formed within him, this disturbance at the time of prayer tended to abate. But we must not over simplify. For there will be disturbances in prayer whose origin is other than that of our lower consciousness. Both the gospels and epistles remind us of forces of evil beyond ourselves. St Paul tells us that we fight, not against flesh and blood but against principalities and powers, against spiritual wickedness in high places. At such times, too, we may draw on fields of psychic force set up by other people far and near. Jung's postulate of a collective unconscious is suggestive here. However this may be, our own rule remains the same, to look to God, to mean God, and to go on meaning God. In standing firm within the storm, accepting its batterings, yet looking beyond it to God himself, the end for which we and all men were created, we are being used by the Spirit to neutralise and disinfect evil whatever its origin—and, even more, to work for its transformation. This is the prayerward aspect of St Paul's completing 'what is lacking in Christ's afflictions for the sake of his body, that is the Church'.

Perhaps in the last quotation you noticed that the writer did not have just a single word such as 'God' or 'love', but a complete phrase, 'Be still and know that I am God', with which to focus his attention. The author of *The Cloud* also commends this. In chapter 7, he gives this tenderly beautiful phrase in the power of which distraction may be overcome, 'Him I covet, Him I seek, and none but Him'. No doubt the author would say here, as he has said of the single word, that we should take whatever sentence God gives us. Our possible choice from the paslms must be almost inexhaustible.

The Cloud tells us that when the conflict is at its height the image of looking over the shoulder to God who is beyond may need to be changed for another better suited to meet the challenge of prayer. We are, the author tells us, to surrender ourselves to God in the hands of our enemies, and he bids us to pay special heed to this suggestion 'for I think that if you try it out it will dissolve every opposition'. The picture might be that of a manacled prisoner, quite helpless and at the mercy of his conqueror, and all that is left for him to do is to give himself over utterly and completely into God's care. 'Why art thou so heavy O my soul, and why art thou so disquieted within me?' When words like that come spontaneously to our lips, that is the moment for complete surrender—not to our state, not to our despondency—but to God in the midst of our state. That also was the psalmist's experience. 'O put thy trust in God, for I will yet give him thanks which is the help of my countenance and my God.'

For an exposition of this trustful surrender, or abandonment as it is more generally called, I shall prefer to turn to the classical spiritual writer on this subject, Père de Caussade, confessor and director to the Sisters of the Visitation in France in the eighteenth century. It will be good to draw briefly on his letters to the Sisters through which the theme of abandonment runs like a golden thread. Advising one Sister he writes that when troublesome thoughts cannot be expelled from the mind—in this case he is speaking of excessive fears—'no other remedy remains but to bear this crucifixion in a spirit of total self-abandonment to the will of God'; and this is saying precisely what *The Cloud* is saying, 'Surrender yourself to God in the hands of your enemies'. There is of course in this the perception of faith—not feeling, for 'clouds and darkness are round about us'—that God is holding on to us at this time, never more perhaps than now. You may have the picture of the cat holding her kitten in her mouth and making her way through the undergrowth. The journey may be a painful one leading through thorns and briars, but the small creature knows she is being held. The picture illustrates the passive side of the life of the spirit. It needs to be balanced at other times by the active side, and here we need the picture of the baby monkey, who is not held but clings for dear life to its mother as she makes great leaps from tree to tree. Even so is the Christian's life a holding on until we move into the knowledge that we are being held.

In all his many letters to the Sisters, de Caussade is never in the least alarmed at the afflictions they are called upon to bear. He writes to another Sister, 'I will end this letter by telling you your state is truly crucifying and for that reason sound, desirable, purifying and sanctifying.' He has already told her that the interior fever which seems to destroy her is indeed only destroying the impure and earthly elements, much as the various poisons of the body are destroyed during the crisis of illness. This, he adds, is a sign of recovery and not of sickness. And this is just what it is: de Caussade is not talking here of the healing of the body but of the soul, or if we prefer, the total healing of the whole man, and in modern language we should say that in this standing within the storm in patient endurance with faith unbroken, the personality is being integrated, the disharmonies of our nature are being brought into one harmonious whole; we are being taken on by the Spirit to a fuller maturity in Christ, which in its turn makes possible a deeper relationship in love.

This healing process, naturally, is not to be restricted to the time of prayer. What is begun or comes to special prominence in our prayer life will be taken forward in all our occupations. For the man whose life is immersed in the love and will of God in prayer, the healing will continue through the whole round of life—his work and recreation, his eating and drinking and sleeping, his family relationships, his serving of others, and being served by them. Further we must see this healing process not just as something taking place within ourselves. In it in some degree the healing of all men is caught up. We cannot separate ourselves as though we were each one little islands set here and there in a universal sea. We need an organic picture such as St Paul gives us of the body, where the healthy functioning of each part has its effect for good on the body as a whole.

Here then is our liberation, and in its measure contained within it is the liberation of all. You may know those undying words on the tombstone of Martin Luther King, 'Free at last. Free at last. Thank God Almighty, I am free at last'. Man longs for his full liberation, for liberation and the capacity for love go forward hand in hand. For the opposite of liberty is bondage, and bondage means fear; and it is, as St John tells us, perfect love that casts out fear. That is to say, perfect love liberates, and I am sure we may say liberation makes possible the perfection of love. For purposes known only to God our liberation may often be delayed, finding its perfection only after passing through the gate of death and resurrection. We can only place ourselves in the hands of the Spirit, content to be taken on at his pace, believing that God's purposes are best served in ourselves and through ourselves to those around us by our being re-fashioned in his time and not in ours. Meanwhile our infirmities, and oddities, and annoyances, and quirks remain, serving not only to humble us, but perhaps to present the sort of challenge to those around us which each needs from the other, until at the last we are brought, in St Paul's undying words, to 'the glorious liberty which belongs to the children of God'.

Chapter 4

THE PRACTICE OF CONTEMPLATION

Finally, I want above all things to be practical. We have examined *The Cloud* together, or at least the heart of its teaching, and we have learnt in some measure how we are to proceed in the prayer of contemplation, and how to deal with the memories and imaginations which threaten to defeat us at this time. Let us now imagine that we are coming to our time of prayer.

First let me ask why we are coming. We are coming because we believe in a general way that this is the form of prayer to which the Holy Spirit is calling us. We have already examined the signs of that call and we need not refer to them again now. But we are coming too because this is our time of prayer, the occasion of our offering. We are not coming because we feel like praying. It may be that we do. It is more likely that we do not, and it is possible that prayer is about the last thing in the world that we feel like doing. It is essential that we get this clear. To be ruled by feeling, by sense impression is a mark of spiritual immaturity. The mature are ruled by faith. Every act of prayer is an act of faith. Father de Caussade wrote in *Abandonment to the Divine Providence,* 'Faith is nothing else than a continual pursuit of God through everything that disguises, misrepresents, and so to speak annihilates him.' Is that not exactly what our feelings, our sense impressions, whether gathered from external events or from the internal vageries of the body, are continually doing? If in that great drama of the Old Testament Job, deprived of his possessions, bereaved of his children, and afflicted with suffering, had relied on what he saw and heard and felt, he would have taken his wife's advice and cursed God and died. Only the eye of faith could penetrate the cloud of afflicting sense experience and cry out 'though he slay me yet will I trust him'. So too when feelings are against us, whether before prayer or during prayer, it is only by acts of faith that we can reject them for the fraud they are and pursue our appointed way. Nor should we complain that this is so. We ought rather to rejoice, for every temptation to deny prayer on account of feeling carries within it the opportunity for a growth of faith. Archbishop Temple once said that if we prayed for patience, we must expect God to answer our prayer by giving us opportunities in which to exercise it. The same principle is true if we pray for faith or, for that matter, for any grace. This is the moment when faith is nourished and quickened, and never more so than when mood and feeling are against us. C. S. Lewis once defined faith as the holding on to what reason has accepted in spite of changing moods. It was, he said, the telling mood and emotion where they got off when they threatened to carry out a blitz on the reason. In the life of the spirit there has to be a stripping of the senses which involves throwing the whole burden on faith, not because the senses are evil—no one who believes in the Incarnation can accept that—but because they are so supremely good that neither God nor man can be satisfied with anything less than the realisation of their full potential. And that can come about only through the cleansing process—the pruning of the vine that it may bear more fruit—of which a part is effected in prayer informed by faith at those times when the senses are being deprived of what they are most wanting. As St John of the Cross tells us, man has to be led from the position in which his will rests and feeds on sense experience, not (ultimately) to the denial of the joys of sense, but to a liberty of spirit in the midst of such joys. This is the true joy for which we were created, and the arid and night experiences of prayer prepare us for it both by what the Spirit effects within us at the time, and by creating (again in the power of the Spirit) the dispositions which will enable us to meet the disciplines of life, so that they can be used by him as the agent for the completion of what remains to be done.

Yet there will undoubtedly be days when we shall need the support of a book in helping us through the difficult seasons of prayer. We are like children learning to walk, and we need a rail to hold and to return to after each unaided trial. It is better frankly to acknowledge and accept this need than to persevere in a way which may for the present be too hard for us. Spiritual reading, as it is normally called, differs from discursive meditation in that the mind and the imagination are now channelled very simply to the words or sentences before us. We do not think around our subject but accept each passage as it comes, and allow it 'to dissolve in the mind as a sweet dissolves in the mouth'. The quotation is from de Caussade and could scarcely be bettered, though as always what the mind feeds on is to descend to the heart. We read the passage slowly, extracting the flavour of each sentence before we allow ourselves to go on to the next. A minute or much longer may pass between the successive pauses. It should not worry us if there are times when the whole period of prayer is passed in this way. But as soon as we find that further reading is coming in the way of a fuller silence, the book will be laid aside to be returned to later if desired. Until that time our reading gives the mind and imagination just that amount of material on which it needs to feed. This is not different in principle from the one word 'firmly fixed to the heart', or the single sentence allowed by *The Cloud*. Spiritual reading is performing the same function at one stage earlier, allowing the mind and imagination more diversity than in the case of the single word or sentence. The passage needs to be chosen with care. Anything which stimulates intellectual excitement or curiosity is worse than useless. For that reason well-known readings are likely to be most suitable. We are not then eager to see how the theme ends, for this we already know. It will be best that we find our own books as the Spirit ministers to our varying needs. Psalms and hymns and some books of prayer lend themselves specially to sentence by sentence reading with frequent pauses. The letters of such masters of the spiritual life as St Francis de Sâles, de Caussade, Fénelon and others allow for longer readings between each break; or spiritual classics such as *The Confessions of St Augustine, The Imitation of Christ* or other works ancient or modern may be used.

Secondly, for how long are we here? I do not think we shall ever get far unless we fix a definite time; even if in practice it sometimes has to be cut short. For people who live alone like myself it is almost presumptuous to make suggestions to the busy housewife. But I should like to suggest we do not overlook the possibility of keeping the prayer time in church so that we can be relatively free from the noise and disturbance. Also group meetings whether in church or elsewhere may be a great help. We support one another in the silence, are encouraged to be regular, and the temptation to cut the time short is eliminated. This seems to be the way in which the Holy Spirit is calling people today.

Then thirdly, in what state have we come? Are we perhaps tense and keyed up? We do not go to prayer that we may become relaxed (though we shall find that it will have this effect upon us). However, if we are tense, it is doubtful if we shall ever have the resolution to begin. We need a phasing-in period. In the East it is common to see yoga so used. The taking up of the various postures assists in a releasing of tensions which leads the disciple to the stillness of meditation. Some are discovering this in the West (though I do not refer to the schools of yoga which use it as a bodily discipline cut off from its spiritual roots). But there are other ways of 'phasing-in', and we probably know where we shall find our own. Someone not long ago described hers, in a published article, as gardening; or it may be knitting, or weaving, or music, or taking a walk round the garden. What is common to these activities, if the right one has been chosen, is that they will be relaxing the body and mind.

Do not forget that vocal prayer of the sort earlier described may also be a way in; so may simple relaxation. Indeed to spend the first few minutes at the start of prayer in an act of relaxation may often be the best way to begin. We hear a good deal about relaxation nowadays, and bearing in mind its close relationship with prayer perhaps I should say something about it. First, what the word does *not* mean. Relaxation does not mean lazing away one's time in idleness. As a working definition, I would suggest that a relaxed state is 'a state of creative awareness "through the lessening and elimination of mis-directed tension and effort'". The second part of that phrase I have taken from a brochure of Ursula Fleming, a teacher of relaxation (though I should prefer to call her art 'creative relaxation'), who goes on to describe it as 'a way of growth both in the life of prayer and into a fuller humanity'. The primary dictionary definition of the word is taken up with such words as loosening, slackening, reducing tension. That is too negative for our purpose. When I use the word, will you always add to its ordinary meaning the positive conception of creative awareness?

It may be best to approach the subject from the point of view of human relationships. Have you ever known yourself to say 'I enjoy spending an evening with X. I always come home so refreshed and relaxed'? Yet the reason for your visit was not that you might become relaxed but that you might know your friend better, and take pleasure in his company and conversation. That you return relaxed is a by-product of the event. And does it not by analogy ring true, that if we are in prayer truly in touch with the creative love and being of God, we shall emerge fresh and relaxed? But the illustration does not end there. Might you not on occasion equally have to say 'My time with my friend yesterday was quite different from before. I was so tense when I arrived that I was unable to absorb all that he was waiting to give me'? And if you said that, you might add that next time you visit him you will relax first, that you might experience the full benefit of his company. Surely this too can be applied to prayer? We can be so tense when we go to prayer that we can no more establish rapport with the Spirit, or he with us, than we could truly meet our friend on that unfortunate evening. So it makes sense to say that when we feel tense before prayer we shall first relax that we may become more receptive to what the Spirit would give us. Prayer is not relaxation, and relaxation is not prayer, but for the Christian there exists a vital partnership between the two. And if in the way of the Spirit's leading, you say that you are now going to relax for the love of God, you are doing something at least as close to prayer as if you say you will garden for the love of God, or that you will knit for the love of God. And all three, and other similar activities, have this, we note, in common that they will be relaxing to mind and body and hence be ways in to prayer.

Relaxation does not mean as someone described it to me the other day 'going all of a flop'. It does not mean doing nothing. It certainly may look to others that you are doing nothing, and you may on occasions wonder the same thing yourself. I sometimes say to people who think that in prayer they are doing nothing, then for this once stop praying and *really* do nothing—make yourself a cup of tea and sink back into an arm chair and let the mind go where it will. You will see how easy it is, and hence you will deduce how hard you must have been working before. You could say just the same about relaxation. Even after a person has accepted the idea of relaxation, its practice will call for a similar courage and resolution as that of prayer itself.

Yet we should proceed cautiously, and before we leave this subject it ought perhaps to be said that relaxation is not, as popular articles may sometimes suggest, in itself a magic cure for all our troubles. The truth is, surely, that relaxation *per se* is an a-moral quality; taken in itself it is neither good nor bad. In this respect it may be compared with sleep. Relaxation has the same function as sleep in enabling a work to be more effectively performed, and this independently of the moral worth of the action. Yet to this I would add that I suspect that relaxation (and sleep too) in its proper measure has a built in tendency towards goodness. However this may be, it must be remembered that everything I am saying is built on the supposition that we are seeking the fuller knowledge of God and his will and purpose in our lives, and it is within this context that we are speaking of our subject. We are considering relaxation in relationship to prayer, and prayer as always in relationship to living. And we remind ourselves that the form of prayer of which we are speaking is only allowed by *The Cloud of Unknowing* to those who are seeking to put on the fullness of Christ, being themselves specially called to this way.

I have before me as I write a brochure for a course on relaxation in relationship to prayer. I should like to quote from it these words written by a sister of a contemplative order. 'Relaxation is a means to prayer. To relax is to be able to concentrate on (that is to say to be aware of, to attend to, to accept) the reality of the present; in oneself as a whole first; then in relation to others, to creation, to God.' And then she goes on to say that this concentration of which she has spoken is not a tension of the mind, but an attention to the reality of the present moment. 'It is a relaxing activity. It has to be exercised every day if it is to develop, but it is worth while since it is the door to our communion with God and our neighbour.'

And then fourthly, how about posture in prayer? We pray as whole persons not as spirits, nor yet as spirits within a body as water might be thought of within a bottle, but as a body-soul-spirit complex. To neglect the place of the body would be a denial of that side of our nature of which we are for the most part most conscious. It is only sensible if we want to go to sleep that we take up the posture most suited to sleep. So too in prayer we take up the position the body would tend to find of its own accord if when praying it were left to itself. The author of *The Cloud* discovered the position for himself and perhaps we have done the same.

The basic thing about posture is that the back shall be straight and held in an easy tension. This may be so whether we stand, or sit on an upright chair, or kneel upright, or kneel sitting on the heels (a cushion placed on the heels can be a help here for some), or kneel with the help of a prayer stool, or sit on the floor lotus fashion with legs crossed and feet tucked under the body. This last is an inadvisable posture in the West except for those who have trained themselves to hold it easily. The rule should be to assume whichever position we can maintain without undue strain. Let us assume we choose to sit on an upright chair. First the back will be straight. This position held in an easy tension will assist a natural counter relaxation of the temples and forehead muscles of the face and jaw. The mouth should be shut but not tightly so. The eyes will be closed, eyeballs down and relaxed and we look mentally to the heart. The arms too will be relaxed with hands resting relaxedly, palms downwards on the upper parts of the thighs, or in the lap, palms upwards. I believe there is value in saying and knowing these things, but I do not want to be over assertive in this matter. I have great respect for *The Cloud* approach of putting down no rules but simply allowing the body to straighten out naturally to its correct position as the prayer proceeds. Yet I am sure we need this other approach too, It must be left to the individual to find the right balance between the two. The classic position for the head is erect, firmly set on the neck; the back, neck, and head forming one straight line. Some find that when the head is slightly inclined forward it assists in mentally looking at the heart. You will notice how often we come back to this. 'Draw the mind through the heart', the Orthodox say. Let your word ('God', 'love', or whatever it may be) 'be firmly fixed to the heart', says *The Cloud*.

Of course we are not so silly as to believe that by adopting the most meticulously correct position we are now at prayer. All we are doing is to attempt to assist the Spirit in his work. I have described only the skeleton, the dry bones of the valley, which the Spirit must breathe upon and clothe with flesh if they are to live. Or we are like the servants at the wedding feast who were told to fill the water pots with water. Only the Lord of life can turn it into wine.

We now move on to the prayer itself. Will you picture three concentric circles? On the circumference of the outer circle I want you to see written, *seeing, hearing, touching, tasting, smelling*—our five senses. Also written on this outer circle will you see written *imagination* and *memory*, and lastly on the same circle *intellect* and *will*. The space outside the circle stands for the world of everyday affairs, and these nine faculties which we see written on the circumference are to be understood in their normal relationships to the happenings which go on around us. As the Spirit enables us to pray, we leave this outer circle behind and move to the circumference of the middle circle. And with us we shall take *memory* and *imagination* and also *intellect* and *will* but not the five senses. These are left behind, so will you cross them out on the outer circle?—but cross them out in pencil, because we shall later come back to them. I say we leave behind the five senses. That is easiest to see in relationship to sight. In prayer we close our eyes and so shut out the visual sense altogehter. We cannot in the same direct physical way shut out the other senses. For example, if a car passes on the road we cannot escape hearing it, but so far as we can we do not give attention to it.

Here then we are on the middle circle, and now we have to deal with memory and imagination. We can think of these as one. Memory is really a part of imagination. When our imagination is aware of something which happened to us in the past we call it memory. When we simply imagine something outside our own experience, then that is pure imagination and memory plays no part. Also, only imagination can have reference to the future. We can think of these two faculties under one head. St John of the Cross likens them to a sixth sense, and it is not difficult to see how this is so. We may close our eyes and shut out all seeing, but we can still with the imagination 'see' our car in the parking place outside. We even have a phrase for it in the English language, 'seeing with the mind's eye' which exactly expresses St John of the Cross' meaning. In the same way if you are musical you may be able, if I may coin the phrase, 'to hear with the mind's ear' playing back to yourself through the imagination some favourite concerto you have enjoyed. People who stand all agog in the queue for fish and chips may be said 'to be tasting with the mind's palate'. The idea is clear and I need not make the point with the other senses. You will see at once where our line of thought is taking us. If it makes sense in prayer to cut out *seeing,* and we shall probably all agree that it does, for it is a generally accepted custom to close the eyes in prayer, then it makes no sense at all to retain the faculty of 'seeing with the mind's eye', that is to say, to use the imagination to recapture the sense of sight. It makes no sense to bolt the doors of the senses against the thief if you leave the windows of memory and imagination open. Either we leave the house open or we close it altogether. It will be clear that the argument we have used with regard to sight in relationship to imagination is equally valid in the realm of hearing and imagination, or of touching, tasting and smelling on the one hand, and imagination on the other.

Why then am I making this point? It is to reinforce the teaching of *The Cloud. The Cloud,* as we have seen, tells us not only to look to the cloud of unknowing before us, but to put down the cloud of forgetting beneath us. Memories and imaginations are to be resolutely stepped over, or, to use another metaphor, we are to seek to look over their shoulder to God who is beyond. And having illustrated as we have done that memory and imagination are a sixth sense, what we have called windows through which the thief may enter after we have locked all the five doors of the house, we are in a position to see why the teaching of *The Cloud* must be as it is, and could not indeed be otherwise. And that is a point gained, because whilst everyone accepts that it is quite reasonable to cut oneself off from sight in prayer, and to pray if possible away from disturbing noise, and to act similarly with regard to the other senses, yet when it comes to this question of leaving behind memory and imagination, they ask perhaps whether this is not taking things a little too far. But we have seen that if we attend to these two faculties we might just as well attend to the five senses, and we know that to do that would be disastrous.

But we are still on this middle circle and now we move into the inner circle, crossing out memory and imagination (in pencil for we shall come back to them), and I hope that after what I have said you will be quite content to let them go. To the circumference of this inner circle we bring *intellect* and *will*. 'Intellect' is now to be understood not in its discursive form, but as ability to know by intuition without reasoning, and 'will' is to be understood as ability to love by a single act and not by a multiplicity of acts as is normal in everyday life. (Cf. Hoffman, *The Life Within*, page 12.)

Here then the Holy Spirit has brought us to the heart of our prayer. In terms of *The Cloud*, we are to lift up our hearts to God, with humble love to mean God, to hate to think of anything but God, to try to forget all created things, to strike the thick black cloud of unknowing with the sharp dart of longing love, and on no account to think of giving up. A short word such as 'God' or 'love' may be used as a focal point for the mind. This 'fixed firmly in the heart' is to be 'our shield and spear'.

Yet we know only too well that memory and imagination, although we have crossed them out as a sign that they have been left behind, will be continually trying to force their way in and to divert our attention from this our work of prayer. What then are we to do, when despite our desire to attend to God and to him alone, we perceive these things trying to gain a foothold within us? Certainly we are not to fear. If the will remains constant they can do us no harm. Or more positively they can become the means of strengthening the will in its resolution to mean God and him alone. *The Cloud* has spoken of looking over their shoulder to God. Let me give you another picture I have found helpful. Will you imagine that you are taking a motor launch up a river, and your eye is on the goal you want to reach, which in our illustration stands for God? Coming down the stream and floating by is all sorts of bits of rubbish, bits of wood from broken up packing cases, empty tins and bottles and soggy paper thrown overboard by picnic parties, flotsam and jetsam of every kind. These of course represent the memories and distracting thoughts which may float across the mind and seek to gain admission during prayer. What are we to do with them? We are simply to let them float past us, keeping our eye upon the goal. *Floating,* you will know, is a word frequently used in practical psychology. Let your anxieties float, we are told. And all this rubbish is to float. We are not to fix our eyes on it—our eyes are on the goal—yet we know that often we cannot but be aware of it out of the corner of our eye as it slips silently by. We may be tempted to turn and look at it, but to do that in the time of prayer will not help but hinder. We may be tempted yet more to examine it, and that would hinder even more. Worst of all we may be tempted to put our hands over the side of the boat and bring some of it aboard. If we do that our prayer time is finished. Our position with regard to this rubbish is a neutral one. We do not encourage it and we do not run away from it. We simply pass on our way through it. It is in this standing within the storm within the experience of prayer, looking to God and meaning God and him alone that our healing is taking place. We have already seen in the last chapter that we cannot separate our healing from that of others. All mankind is in a measure caught up in what is being done. This standing within the conflict is most truly a work of intercession, a work of reconciliation between God and man—that is to say all men, in which I myself am included.

The world and the devil may have their part in this rubbish which is floating by. But much of it will be of the flesh—my flesh—using the word to stand for the whole lower nature: pride, anger, jealousy, taking their place with gluttony and lust. Memories may float by, the subconscious or unconscious may throw up material repressed or partially repressed, often disguised, as dreams disguise the lower levels of the mind. Here is the carcase of a cat floating towards us, a pretty smelly piece of garbage this, and we shall get a whiff of it as it goes by. But never mind, it won't kill us. We remain constant, looking to God our redeemer and saviour in Christ, as Peter looked to Jesus as he walked across the stormy water; or rather, we remember that it was when he ceased to look that he began to sink. There will be suffering, yes, but it will be creative suffering, the suffering of purgation and cleansing. It is the place of healing, the place where the Spirit is bringing our disintegrated personalities into one harmonious whole. We may not know it at the time, but later we shall be able to say with Jacob, 'Surely the Lord is in this place and I knew it not'.

Every illustration is likely to break down at one point or another, and in passing we may note two weaknesses in the one we have given. We have said that in taking our boat up-stream our eye is to be on the goal which we wish to reach, and that that goal is God. This, however, gives a 'God-out-there' image which is not helpful for our purpose. We have already stressed that in our prayer we shall do well always to be looking mentally towards the heart. The limits imposed by our example must not mislead us here. The second weakness in our illustration is that it suggests that only painful or disagreeable or worthless things will tend to occupy the imagination in our prayer time. This, as we have seen, is by no means true. It would clearly have been unrealistic to have included precious stones amongst the rubbish passing by, especially if we had tried to make them float! Memories of what is good and pleasing will also seek to claim our attention, but whatever their nature they are to be covered 'with a thick cloud of forgetting'. The point to grasp is that *all* memories, imaginations and considerations will be *as dross for our purpose at this time.* To attend selectively to some 'when they are holy and promise well' would be to make us as prisoners whose liberty is equally curtailed whether the rope which binds us is of silk or of rough hemp.

Father de Caussade has another picture which may help us at such times. He says we are simply to allow these memories and distractions to drop away as you might let stones drop into the sea. We are to resist them by concentrating on contrary reflections, turning to God to make new acts of trust and abandonment. We are ever to plunge ourselves anew into the ocean of God's love. Fénelon calls this forgetting of self the most perfect penitence 'because all conversion consists only in renouncing self to be engrossed in God'.

But we are not to be worried if our distractions do not drop away as we might wish. Sometimes these stones which are to fall into the sea appear to be more like rubber balls which float around us. What matters is that the attitude of the will is one of letting go. The open hand is the symbol here. The very act of opening the hand helps us to let go with the mind. We may encourage ourselves with the old Chinese proverb, 'You cannot prevent birds flying around your head, but you can prevent them making nests in your hair'.

And now our prayer time is over. What is it we have been doing? If you like, we have been taking a holiday. If that sounds an odd thing to say, let us not forget that holidays mean doing hard and challenging things like climbing mountains or exploring unknown country. But this has been the best sort of holiday, for not only have we got away from it all, which is essential on any holiday, but we have been in touch with the fount of all life, and so have found *re*-creation of body, mind, and spirit. We know how important it is for us to get away from our work from time to time, not that we may neglect it but that we may see it in the perspective of eternity. And so we return to our work as before, and yet not as before, for in this prayer the Holy Spirit has reached down to the subliminal depths of our being, cleansed us, purified us, helped to unify us and to integrate the various sides of our nature, so that we may bring to our work a deeper integrity, a clearer perception of the real needs of those around us, a fuller understanding of the fears and tensions which threaten to overwhelm others as we come to grips with these things within ourselves, and a love disciplined and made strong through an ever deeper union with God himself.

EPILOGUE

'Love is my meaning.' The words are taken from the title of a recent anthology, in itself a quotation from Mother Julian. Love holds the key to all that has been said, and to all that can be said whatever the nature of our calling in prayer. No method of prayer can of itself be valid apart from this dimension of love. In prayer love is expressed and deepened, and yet more it is refashioned, as in an ever renewed dying and rising again it takes its form from the wisdom and perfection of God. The saints are the great lovers, but it is God's love which is shed abroad in their hearts, and no other love than God's redeeming and saving love will avail. 'At eventide they will examine you in love.' So wrote St John of the Cross, and the quotation is commonly ended there. We need perhaps to reflect that he at once went on to say that it is not the human love of our natural temperament of which he speaks, but of that which is of the nature of God's own love. And this he describes elsewhere as a living flame which tenderly wounds the soul at its deepest centre. What a corrective is this to our own poor human notions, often more sentimental than strong, more possessive than pure, more spoiling than wise, more tolerant than true. How well would St John of the Cross have understood, and we too shall grow to understand, the saying which tradition has attributed to Jesus, 'He that is near me is near the fire'!

FAIRACRES PUBLICATIONS

PUBLICATIONS BY GILBERT SHAW

POSTAGE EXTRA. All publications listed above are obtainable from:

SLG Press, Convent of the Incarnation, Fairacres, OXFORD, OX4 1TB